Love's Seasons
By Tremayne Moore & Stephanie Tysor

Published by Maynetre Manuscripts, LLC

ISBN Number: 0-9960743-2-5 (Paperback)
ISBN Number: 0-9960743-3-3 (eBook)

Printed in the United States of America
First Printing 2018
10 9 8 7 6 5 4 3 2 1

Edited by: Makasha Dorsey & Cynthia M. Portalatin
Cover design created by DGPR, LLC

Love's Seasons

By Tremayne Moore & Stephanie Tysor

Introduction

Before you enter this journey that will cause an encounter you'll never forget, we would like to take a moment to share a little bit about us and how this project got started.

Back in 1983, we were next-door neighbors living in Fort Meade, Maryland. It was only a matter of a time before our respective families took on an extended family. We attended the same school, even though I was one grade ahead of Stephanie. At the time, I was in 4th grade, and she was in 3rd grade. Her older brother was in the same grade with me, and we became best friends until my family left for Germany in 1989, as my late father received orders to move.

I believe if Stephanie could describe me in the 80s, obnoxious might be an understatement. If I could describe her in the 80s, she'd definitely be the "littler sister" who tagged along. Apart from that, she had a spirit as such you'd see of a caterpillar swiftly becoming a butterfly.

Through social media, we found each other again. By that time, I had already released a book or two. One day in 2012, she typed a poem on her wall, and I felt that it required a response. That emerged into the poem entitled "Can You?" (Final Mixdown). From that point, we wrote poems in real-time, on our respective Facebook (FB) walls, requiring people to get inside their minds as they tried to come up with eight lines within a 10-minute period.

Every poem you will read in this book – with the exception of the interludes - was written "live" on FB. We pray that you enjoy them.

Tremayne Moore

Stephanie Tysor – mother, daughter and sister – I am a native of Hampton, Virginia. I was born to Sandra Tysor and the late Thomas Tysor. My father was in the military, and I of course was what we call a "military brat." We were fortunate to spend the majority of our time in one place. I spent time on Ft. Meade and Severn, Maryland until my father retired from the United States Air Force. Once I left Maryland, I moved to Virginia where I still reside.

Reading and writing poems has always been a favorite pastime for me. Writing allows me to express my inner thoughts. Writing is a form of therapy when I feel overwhelmed. However, writing does not just articulate my feelings; it also communicates emotions others are feeling.

As Tremayne stated, we have known each other since the 80s. Being the "little sister," of course, I thought he was "obnoxious" (smile). However, I wouldn't change anything about him. I am so very thankful we reconnected through social media. Through our love of music and poetry we have been able to create what I believe is a collection of words that can and will touch each of you in some way.

Stephanie Tysor

Note

As you read this book, we desire to help you differentiate who wrote each section. With the exception of the interludes, Tremayne's verses are not italicized, and Stephanie's verses are italicized.

Dedication

We dedicate this book in the loving memory of our respective fathers:

Harry Moore
Thomas Tysor

Table of Contents

Love's Season #1: Spring

Something In Our Hearts
Written May 2, 2012

Honey, I see no reason why we should be apart.
Because when we first met,
     an angel appeared to our hearts.
After the appearance, something was in my heart,
     and your heart as well.
We were hooked on each other,
     and it was so easy to tell.
Months later, you've seen the changes
     I've gone through in my life.
Your love has touched my spirit,
     removing my past pain and strife.
It feels like we've known each other
     since we were in our teens.
But here we stand today, and
     I just want you to be my queen.

Each day with you feels like the first.
I am thankful for every minute
     in your love I am immersed.
These feelings are deep;
     they are strong;
     they are real.
There are not enough words to express how I feel.
Everyone walking by can see the love that we share.
It is in our gazes,
     in our touch,
     simply in the air.
I feel in my heart I have known you all my life.
I am at that point where
     I am hoping you will make me your wife.
You see; when I look at you
     I know I have found my king.
My heart and love are on the line,

anything you want is for the taking.

If we were birds,
         we could soar the heavens together.
All I know is that it would be you and I forever.
Daydreaming of you gets me through my day.
The sound of your name points me your way.
I want to be with you only,
         and no one could tell me otherwise.
Let's talk right now about a wedding date,
         now that should take you by surprise.
My heart and love are on the line as well,
         and I want all my feelings to show
that I'm all yours; from this day forth,
         this is something you should know.

Hand-in-hand as we soar through the clouds above,
my heart bursts with an abundance of love.
Your voice is what does it for me.
Just hearing you say "hello"
         speeds up my pulse and makes me giddy.
Setting a wedding date —
         is that what you want to do?
This is quite a surprise;
         this is something to which I had no clue.
However, I know I am ready
         to spend the rest of my life with you.
There is no one else in this world
         who elicits the love that I have for you.
Never doubt me or my feelings,
         because my actions will show and prove
that my love for you is here to stay.
         Together there is nothing we can't do.

When you hold me tight,
         my heart races through space.
To feel your breath on my face

takes me to another place.
To hear my name across your lips
        makes my world stop for you.
No woman can hypnotize me the way that you do.
I'm glad you're surprised;
        that was all part of my plan.
Now that we are committed,
        let me pick you up.
        I promise to be a gentleman.
I will never doubt you or your feelings,
        and I ask that you promise me the same.
The last thing I want is for our friends
        to think this relationship is a game.

No games played here;
        this is something you never have to fear.
Our love is real. It shows in our actions;
        that much is clear.
I love that your heart races when I hold you tight.
I plan on holding on tight each and every night.
I have no idea
        how you came along and mesmerized me.
But when you walk in a room,
        my heart races steadily.
I pledge to you from this moment on
        to be the woman you desire.
For the greatest love of all
        is something to which I aspire.

I vow to be the man you dream of, but
        more importantly,
        to be what God wants me to be.
I want to assist you with bringing your gifts to pass,
        and I pray you do the same for me.
There are so many things
        your presence does to this man.
Now this dream of mine is real,

and I put my heart into your hands.
I don't believe in coincidences as to how we met.
All I know is that we're here together, and
      our meeting is something we'll never forget.
Let's go shop for a ring,
      though no ring can match your worth to me.
I know we'll never be lonely,
      for our two lonely hearts have been set free.

Can You (Final Mixdown)
Written March 8, 2012

Can you be that person I need when I call?
Never putting me on hold,
        no one coming before me at all.
Can you say I'm your heart
        and really mean it?
And, not just tell me,
        but show me with your actions
        and the time spent.
Can you say, when its time, you can give me your all?
I'm an original, unlike no other, remember this...
        I am me.
        I shall never fall.
Can you say that your words are the truth?
        That you speak no lies?
Think before you speak;
        I can see the truth in your eyes.
Can we shut out the world for just one day?
No errant thoughts to go astray.
Can you honestly say you can handle a strong
        woman?
One who may bend but can never be broken?
Can you be a One-Woman Man?
Coming home every night,
        never running the streets like a mad man.
Can you be that man a woman can trust?
        Not just a man that is here out of lust?
Can you...
Can you be that MAN?
        That man who makes all women sit up
        and pay attention,
But be that one and only man
        who doesn't play anymore,
        because home is one-in-a-million!

Can you be that woman
     who can feel me when I call?
Or, are you the type of woman,
     that's all or nothing at all?
Can you say that you love me
     and really mean it?
Not just by you kissing me, but
     treasuring all our time spent.
Can you say that...
     you're not trying to manipulate me just
     for your selfish reasons?
I want the best for the both of our spirits and,
     more importantly, to love you
     for all seasons.
Can you actually look me in the eyes
     and say you're telling me pretty lies?
I'm not as gullible as you think I am.
     I can discern your thoughts
     when I look in your cinnamon eyes.
Can we just go for a romantic drive...
     for just one day?
Walk together on the beach,
     holding hands
     without having anything to say,
Can you honestly say
     you can handle a faithful man?
     Who is all about serving the Lord
     the best way he can?
Can you handle this One-Woman Man?
     Who is loyal and faithful to you and
     will place his entire life into your hands?
Honey, I can be that man, the one you can trust.
I want you for life, not just
     to be with you to satisfy our lusts.
I can give you this ring, and there's one more thing
     I need to mention.
My life is yours, and yours is mine, and
     you have my undivided attention!

Now that I have your attention,
     and your intentions have been made
I accept your ring on my hand;
     It's my heart you have saved.
Through our faith in the Lord,
     I can handle a faithful man.
I am ready to hold on to your hand,
     the one grasped firmly into mine.
We can walk on a beach hand-in-hand any day—
     not just one.
I'm here when you need me,
     always eager to listen
     to what you have to say.
No longer asking,
     can you.
Now, I know our feelings are real,
     and our love will continuously be shown.

Patiently Waiting (Remix)
Written March 9, 2012

They say, "the best things come
        to those who wait."
Loneliness is a feeling I can't seem to shake.
I sit back patiently awaiting my Prince,
        because I know that through my faith
        I must have patience.
Nothing good comes easy—this I know,
So, again I will sit and patiently wait for him to show.
Going through life doing what I must.
No more complaining no time to fuss.
I am a phenomenal woman; look and pay attention.
        I'm only going to say it once.
        So, make sure you listen.
If you don't catch it through what I say,
        then watch my actions, I say.
My miraculous achievements are in all that I do.
        I see it in your reaction,
patiently waiting for you to figure it out.
        Time waits for no one; so, don't miss out.
Your blessing is right in front of you—
        just open your eyes,
Don't wait too long - that might be unwise.
I'm patiently waiting for your games to end,
for that time when your motives
        I no longer must defend.
I'm waiting for a time when
        manipulation doesn't live here anymore.
Waiting, knowing my Prince
        doesn't need to exploit weakness for sure.
Patiently waiting for you to know you have the best,
        you can relax now;
        I have passed all your tests.
Patiently waiting for you
        to realize enough is enough.
Patiently waiting for you
        to know this is love, not lust.
Patiently waiting for you
        to accept this is all about us.
Patiently waiting...

Love's Seasons

We have the rest of our lives to discuss.

They say that good guys always finish last.
Why do we allow this prophecy to come to pass?
Patience is a virtue, as I wait for my Princess.
Every time I close my eyes,
     I see her in a wedding dress.
My life hasn't been easy, and this I know.
     Even though
I'm a man; my feelings are easy to show.
I must travel on this road called life, wondering
     if I'll be old and gray
     before I take on a wife.
I am a well-educated brother;
     my sister, take notice.
If you keep your eyes on thugs,
     you'll lose focus.
I thought my lifestyle proved who I am to you,
please don't allow me to walk out the door
     closing our future as two.
I'm patiently waiting for you to figure it out.
Please lay to rest all your doubts.
Your blessing is in front of you;
     don't miss out.
Take a chance on me,
     'cause you know what I'm about.
I'm patiently waiting for you
     to drop your drama-queen friends.
I know that's a stronghold, but the cycle must end.
I'll declare with you that
     manipulation doesn't, live here anymore.
For you, my Princess, are the one I adore.
I patiently wait for you
     to bring out the best in me.
I accept you in all ways;
     for this is how love should be.
Your wait is over.
     Enough is enough.
Your wait is over.
     It's about love, not lust.
Your wait is over.
     I accept that it's all about us.

Your wait is over.
      We have the rest of our lives to discuss.

You say my wait is over;
      we have the rest of our lives to discuss.
You now know that
      it's about love, not lust.
I've let go of my drama-queen friends;
      I'm ready for it to be just us to the end.
Can you say the same?
      No more time to pretend.
I want to believe
      the manipulation doesn't live here anymore.
No more games, please show me that
      it is I who you adore.
Eons ago, I stopped wanting thugs.
      I need a brother who's a lover, an about-his-business type
of brother.
I'm taking a leap of faith;
      I'm allowing myself to trust.
Don't make me regret I let go of my doubts.
You know who I am,
what I want, and
what I have to give.
Now, prove to me what you're all about.
Our wait is over.
      Enough is enough.
Our wait is over.
      It's about love, not lust.
Our wait is over.
      We accept its now US.
Our wait is over.
      We have the rest of our lives to discuss!

Anything for You
Written March 11, 2012

Honey, there's nothing that I won't do
      to make you smile.
I'll be a clown just for you;
      to see your dimples makes it worthwhile.
You're all that I'll ever want, and
      God has made you for me.
I'm wrapped around your finger;
      you've got me for eternity.
Our bodies belong to each other;
      I intend to cherish yours for life.
Just say we'll be together, and
      I promise to adore you as my wife.
Take me at my word;
take me in your arms and hold me tight.
I want you forever--
      not like most boys who just want one night.

I hear what you're saying,
      and it sounds real good.
You want me for forever,
      but I don't know if I should.
You will do anything
      just to see me smile.
But, baby, all I want
      is for you to make it worth my while.
I love the words you're saying;
      they sound so good to me.
I hope that what we have will last for eternity.
I have no problem giving you my body,
      if you really want it for life.
Just be real when you tell me
      you want me as your wife.
I've decided to take you at your word
      and let you hold me real tight.
I want to be with you forever
      and not just for one night.

Our destination isn't just pleasure;

it's for the rest of our lives.
I intend to be a real man by my actions,
>to keep our love alive.
I want to be all that you want and need,
>apart from the Lord, of course.
I have turned my back on my past life,
>and I have no remorse.
You've got me, and I'll do anything for you,
As long as
>it doesn't compromise my spiritual virtues.
This destination, where we're going,
>you can drive if you choose to.
Just know that all this horizontal love is for you.

I need a man who stimulates my mind,
Not for one, but through the test of time.
I'm intrigued to know you want
>*to share our pleasure for the rest of our lives.*
As long as your actions are real,
>*our love will stay alive.*
Our faith will be our guidance;
>*the Lord will see us through.*
I do not regret my past,
>*because my past led me to you.*
Show me that I have you,
>*never betraying your faith in God.*
Your faith in our Father should make our love easy,
>*not hard.*
I can drive to our destination,
>*as long as you plan to lead.*
Just never leave me alone,
>*and my love I will give you freely.*

I intend to stimulate your mind,
>not just physically, 'cause that wears off.
Mentally, spiritually, emotionally is the focus,
>for a woman's spirit is soft.
I need you to hold me accountable to
>everything I say.
Not only that, I also need
>to make emotional deposits to your spirit

21

every day.
I won't promise you an easy life,
    for life is full of ups and downs.
But as long as we have each other's back,
    we can face the world without frowns.
I will most definitely lead,
    and I'll never leave you alone.
Let's keep our spirits in sync with the Father,
    and we can lead each other
    to our final Home!

Stimulation of the mind is always a must.
I need to know what's in your mind
    to know if your heart I should trust.
I will hold you accountable for all that you say,
because I need your words and actions
    to embrace me every day.
I don't need an easy life, as long as I have you.
Just ensure you are understanding,
    and you continue to love me, too.
Loving each other, walking hand in hand, with our Father's
guidance we will never be alone.
I'm here where you need me;
    I will follow you to our final home.

I promise to tell you all that's on my mind,
    to erase your doubts.
I need to be honest with you all times;
    that's what love is all about.
Thank you for allowing me
    to express myself to you.
Just know that I love you, and
    I hope that you love me, too.

Thinking of You
Written May 11, 2012

Thoughts of you often consume me.
It's not the words you say
>*but in the actions you give, consistently.*
I find myself loving you more and more each day.
This is something I must show you,
>*because my words can't really say*
>*how much you mean to me,*
>*how much I respect you,*
>*how much I've realized*
>*I can't live without you.*
What makes me smile as I sit here
>*and think about you...*
>*is KNOWING you feel this way too!*

As I sit in my office,
>daydreaming of your lovely face,
time passes slowly;
>I'm longing to feel your warm embrace.
Even the words I say can't describe the way I feel.
All I know is that
>your actions are so pure and real.
You're sweet as a caramel Frappuccino,
>soft as a baby's skin.
You never have to worry about my love for you
>wearing thin.
Let's just take the day off
>to spend time in each other's arms.
Who needs work today?
>It's Friday, and I just want your tender charm.

Too bad I'm at work and unable to leave.
These thoughts of you
>*make work hard to achieve.*
Since its Friday, I think I will take an early day.
Look for me around three

coming down the driveway.
There are no words to express how I truly feel.
All I know is these feelings, as you say,
        are pure and real.
I sit here anticipating the moment
        I will see you again.
Because you are not just my lover,
        you are and will always be my best friend.

I can't leave either,
        but it won't stop my thoughts of you.
I'll catch you at three,
        for nothing can come between us two.
I don't know about you...
        I'm tired of living for the weekend.
Working for the man,
        with no time left for me to spend.
We need a plan,
        to make time for our love and our careers.
It's springtime, love is in the air,
        and our love is unequivocally clear.
Just a few more hours 'till
        I see your dimples and smile.
I just need to be patient
        for it will definitely be worthwhile.

I keep watching the clock,
        urging the time to speed up.
As the time ticks by, my heart beat picks up.
Time nor distance can keep us apart;
From the very beginning, you had my heart.
You have a talent — with the world it should be shared.
You no longer have to work for the man,
        because for the world
        you are already prepared.
You've already started to share your thoughts

and your heart with the world.
I am so proud to be known as your girl.
It's time for you to take that plunge,
  make a clean break.
Start working for yourself;
  I am by your side to do whatever it takes.
You see, I believe in you and all that you do.
Our love will inspire you as long as it's just us two.

If I Could Be Where You Are
Written May 14, 2012

If I could be where you are — I'd hold you in my arms tonight,
never to leave your sight,
ensure we never fight, and
take our relationship to another plight.

If I could be where you are —
there'd be nothing or no one
        who could come between us.
The thought of you departing leaves me breathless.
I need you here with me always.
Just tell me that when you get here you will stay.

If I could be where you are —
you'd no longer be in my dreams.
My heart would flow like a stream.
I'd be able to hear your heart beating next to mine,
and knowing that forever awaits us
        makes me feel so fine.

If I could be where you are —
You would feel how much
        I love you in my every touch.
I never knew I would miss you this much.
You would know that our love fulfills me
        in every moment that we share.
My words alone can't express
        the emotions I have for you;
        they can't express how much I care.

If I could be where you are —
there would be no distance between us.
I wouldn't have to sing to myself,
        "I'm so lost without you."
There would be no need to reach out my hand

to touch your lovely face.
And these images of you in my mind,
    I don't have to retrace.

If I could be where you are —
the loneliness I feel would not hurt me so deep.
It wouldn't be so hard for me
        each night to get to sleep.
I would spend the rest of my life
        telling you what you mean to me.
My actions, my words,
        my love would shine through completely.
I would hold on to you from now
        until the end of time.
I fear that this won't happen, and
        you will never be mine.

If I could be where you are —
time wouldn't keep us apart anymore.
I would be able to sleep better than ever before.
It would no longer be winter in my life,
because I know that you will be my wife.
I don't know about you,
        but I need to make this known.
We need each other,
        and in each other's arms is our home.

Would You Mind
Written August 5, 2012

I don't know why
      love has found my heart right now,
but I know there's a way for me to
      explain it, somehow.
I've never felt this way before, but I love how I feel.
I promise to respect our boundaries;
      so, let me be real.
Would you mind
      if I just looked at your beautiful eyes?
Your captivating smile
      always takes me by surprise.
Would you mind
      if I held you for a slow dance tonight?
This love in my heart now just feels right.

I've been waiting forever for love to come my way.
Now that it's here, I hope that it stays.
Never have I felt anything like this before.
All I know is that it is you who I adore.
Each day I sit and wait just for that moment
      I can look in your eyes,
because in them I see the love we share—
      never any lies.
I would love for you to hold me
      for a slow dance tonight,
because only with you does this love feel right.

Would you mind if I tell you how I feel?
I know you don't like fake people;
      so, here's my chance to be real.
I've loved you for a long time;
      it's time to get serious.
You're the woman my heart beats for,
      and I'm so curious
to know if you'll stay with me forever.

I promise you that
this love that I feel isn't temporary,
    and that's a fact.
Knowing that you love me back,
    it sure feels good to me.
Never mind 50/50 love, it's 100 percent both ways,
    like it's supposed to be.

Please, sir, tell me how you feel.
The only way we can be is real.
We have no time to play games,
because I believe what we want
    is one and the same.
I am waiting here with baited breath,
hoping that what you say
    will ease this ache in my chest.
I've loved you for so long now.
I'm hoping true love is what we have now found.

There are times where
    I want to kiss and hold you tight.
I want to be with you for more than just one night.
Tell me how much cash you need
    for your wedding dress?
My money is yours now;
    you aren't a woman I have to impress.
You love me for me,
    and I couldn't ask God for more.
It feels so good to have someone love me
    like never before.
Would you mind if I propose to you
    to confess this love?
I know He loves me, because
    He's missing an angel from above.

Money is not an option,
    for that is not what I am with you for.
Baby, haven't I proven to you that

it is you that I adore?
I want you to hold me tight all day
and each and every night.
Being in your arms gives me a feeling
that everything is right.
My wedding dress will be special
on that specific day; you will see.
When I walk down the aisle,
it will be officially just you and me.
Yes, baby, you can propose to me now,
for our love can be seen by everyone around.

You most definitely proved
how much you adore me.
I'm so blessed that you even care for me.
I will hold you and cherish you till death do us part.
If I haven't told you before, you are my heart.

You didn't need to tell me,
although it's nice to hear.
You are my love now and forever.
I love you, my dear.
Holding you now has been a dream of mine.
I'm so glad you came into my life;
a man like you I never thought I would find.

I'm so glad you're the woman I prayed for.
Believe me when I say that
I couldn't ask God for more.

I asked God for an angel, one sent just for me.
I wasn't sure in what form this angel would come, but then I
met you, and you set my heart free!

What You've Done To Me
Written October 9, 2012

I woke up early to watch the sunrise,
but the sunrise doesn't compare
        to the sparkle in your eyes.
Your beautiful brown eyes take my breath away,
and it gets me off to a wonderful and lovely day.
This day at work is moving so slow;
        thinking of you gets me through.
All my mind is thinking about
        is just being with you.
Look what you've done to me;
        I refuse to let this feeling go.
You lead me to feel this way,
        and I want to let you know.

This day has been moving so very slowly for me.
I keep glancing out the window, wishing
        that the day wasn't steadily creeping.
I catch my breath each time you glance my way.
Loving you has me looking forward to each day.
Every minute of every day is spent thinking of you.
I am imagining the day that we become one,
        no longer two.

Close your eyes honey,
        and you'll see I'm right there.
Let's hold each other closer than we ever dared.
I pray my embrace will indicate,
        after all is said and done,
that you are mine for a lifetime,
        and these two hearts are now one.
God has blessed me with you, after all this time.
I thought I'd never be married,
        but I'm yours, and you are mine.
The ring on your finger is exquisite,

but you are so much more.
You have my devotion,
and I promise to love you like never before.

Holding on to you dearly, never letting go—
We have a lifetime to let our feelings show.
The warmth of your arms, as they surround me,
instills in me a calmness
knowing God sent you to me.
No longer on my own, I have you by my side.
I can't wait for the day you make me your bride.
Not needing a ring for significance,
the gaze in your eyes
shows me so much more.
I love you now and forever more.
On that day we go from two to one,
no one will change our love for each other;
it can never be undone.

If you're ready to elope, I'm down with that plan.
Not just to get you in bed,
I want to be your one-woman man.
I don't think you're convinced
of what you've done to me.
I'm a changed man for the better,
and that's how God planned it to be.
I know you wouldn't lie to me,
and I wouldn't lie to you.
This was a dream to me, but now it has come true.
I hear a symphony in my head,
and this is my chance.
To hold you in my arms as we dance our first dance.

No lies will ever come from me to you.
You are a one-woman man,
and I'm thankful I found you.
We can elope, if that's what you would like to do,

but I want the world to know how much I love you.
You are the man for me,
        no need to keep that to myself.
I want the world to know you were put here for me,
        no longer needing to keep
        my feelings on the shelf.
I can hardly wait to hear our song play;
so we can dance all night,
        me in your arms no more delays.

My Best Friend My Love
Written May 8, 2014

I know we're just friends,
        but I also know
        that you're an angel from above.
If I'm giving up childish thoughts on relationships,
        then I know I'm in love.
Respecting our boundaries,
        I still keep my prayers focused on you.
Not for us to be together,
        but for your healing and your ministry, too.
You've had bad men that scarred you,
        but it's an honor to cover you
        like Christ covers us.
And it's not for selfish reasons,
        for that's the sure way to betray your trust.
I want to be a friend
        Who sticks closer than a brother.
If we let patience have its perfect work,
        then we'll be a blessing to each other.

I love that you want to be my friend
        and not just my love.
Knowing that, I can trust you unlike any other.
I've been hurt, and I am filled with self-doubt;
I find myself wondering what love is really about.
Right now, I need a man in my life,
        who can really be trusted.
Not one whose around,
        because it's his lust that rules him.
You are my best friend, my strength
        and my love.
I'm thankful that you have been sent from above.

Knowing that you're in a vulnerable state,
        I want to erase any doubts in your mind.
I don't want to cause you to stumble,

34

because you're one of a kind.
Don't ever think that you're going to lose me;
  I'm not going anywhere.
Whether we remain friends or start courting,
  you'll always have my love and care.
However long it takes you to heal,
  I'm willing to wait and pray for you,
because I don't want you to love me
  with any restraints,
  but from a heart that's true.
I remember someone said years ago
  that you can't rush love,
and that's especially true
  when it's sent from up above.

I believe you when you say
  that love cannot be rushed.
It's something that must be nurtured;
  no time can say what you must.
We have been friends for years and years,
and you have been here to be my shoulder
  and dry my tears.
I love you as a brother, as my best friend,
  and soon to be lover.
With you in my life I have no need for any others.
My husband should be my best friend,
  and that is who you are.
You have been a part of me
  whether you were near or far.

I can testify that I have no desire
  to flirt like I used to.
I have abandoned my childish ways
  ever since I've found you.
You are my sister, my best friend
  and the love of my life.
I will wait patiently for you,

when you're ready to be my wife.
Thank you for trusting me to be the man
    I said that I would be.
You just don't know how much that means to me.
I know our future isn't going to be always easy,
    but as long as you have my back,
there's nothing we can't conquer,
    and we can stand against any enemy attack!

Thank you for being the man that you are.
The smile I have when I am with you
    makes me think I can reach the stars.
We both have had moments
    of self-doubt and childishness;
but being away from you causes me to think
    about all that we will miss.
From this point forward,
    let's always promise to be truthful.
Let's always put in an extra effort
    to continue to be useful,
never letting others come between us..
What we have is real, what we have is love.

Let's Be Friends
Written June 21, 2014

It's the first day of summer, and it's you that I love.
I know you're with someone,
      but you're an angel from above.
The relationship you're in won't last much longer;
       that just isn't you.
He'll make you love someone else, treating you
      like you see him do!
Sadly, he doesn't know what love is,
      abandoning the relationship for a fling.
You deserve so much better,
      and don't you worry about a thing.
I know you really like me, and I really like you, too.
I'll never have to wonder
      if you will love me like you say you do.

It's the first day of summer,
      and you say love is in the air.
But at this moment in time, I'm not sure I care.
Yes, I like you; this I do not dispute,
but my emotions are all screwed up
      over a man of ill repute.
How do we start something
      when my circumstances need to end?
I just want to know I will not lose my friend.
Tell me our friendship can survive,
      even though I am not ready to love.

You are so beautiful, and I totally get how you feel.
This friendship period is precious, and if anything,
      this friendship is real.
I know your heart has been through a lot,
      and I know you need time to heal.
I promise you that my heart is off the table;

this should show you my commitment seal.
Heaven smiled on me when you entered my life.
No matter how long the wait,
    you are the woman I want as my wife.
I will pray for your healing,
    known scars and unknown scars.
If I keep my prayers focused on you and not on me,
    this friendship will go far.

I'm thankful to have a friend like you in my life.
I can't promise you right now
    that I can be your wife.
What I can promise you, right this moment,
    is that we will be the best of friends.
There is no one who can come between us;
    this friendship will never end.
Just give me some time to find myself again.
I love knowing that you are my best friend.
I never knew what I was missing,
    until you came into my life.
I never knew, until I met you,
    that what I had wasn't right.
I have to learn to love myself first,
to learn that I have more to offer,
    that I am not cursed.

Take all the time you need;
    I would be insane to let you go.
Having said that,
    there's something I need for you to know.
Don't be so hard on yourself
    In putting your timetable
    ahead of the Lord's.
His will is best for both of us,
    and to miss His timing
    is something we both can't afford.
I'm not saying that
    we need to jump into a relationship,

but take it easy on yourself.
Don't beat yourself up
 with the mistakes you've made;
 it's you I adore and no one else.
I love you, thorns and all,
 and I will enjoy
 this friendship time with you.
Just know that if I lost you as a friend,
 I've lost me too.

Thank you for loving me
 and seeing something I don't see myself.
You bring out the best in me,
 you show me I don't need anyone else.
Thank you for being the man you are
 and not pushing the issue.
I love who I become when I am with you.
I couldn't ask for a better friend,
I'm so thankful you are a special man.

I thank you also for loving me,
 and pulling out things
 that I didn't know I had.
I want to walk with you through
 the good and the bad.
It's not a problem waiting for you;
 I have found a good thing.
He has kept me from trifling women
 by keeping me under His wings.
You're a special woman,
 a beautiful angel and such a great friend,
and I pray that I have you 'till the very end!

Love's Season #2: Summer

Brand New Morning
Written April 16, 2012

It's a brand-new morning, and
      I open my eyes.
I climb out of bed and
      open the shades to see the sunrise.
The morning dew on the window pane
      captures my imagination.
I'm captivated by the purple sky,
      the beauty of God's creation.
A part of me wants to wake you, but
      I let you sleep.
My mind reflects on yesterday,
      about the vows we'll keep.
I kiss you on the cheek and say,
      "Good Morning, I Love You."
Your warm embrace fills my heart,
      as you say you love me too.

Waking up to you brings new meaning to me.
I thank God for opening my eyes
      and allowing me to see.
You are a very special man,
      and I'm thankful to have you in my life.
The vows we took yesterday mean the world to me. I'm so
proud to be your wife.
Every day is beautiful with you standing by my side.
No more running away,
      because from you I never need to hide.

Yesterday was a great day,
      to even include last night.
But knowing that I have you 'till our dying breath
      makes everything alright
This morning is special,
      because we start a new day as man and wife.
I hold you in my arms so tight,

because God blessed me with you in my life.
I'm so glad that you see me as God sees me.
I can't even believe that my dreams have become a reality.
Unlike people we know,
      this relationship isn't just for one night.
I don't need candles,
      for your eyes are my guiding light.

Each and every day,
      from here to the end of time,
I will value you and your love,
      knowing that I am yours, and you are mine.
This morning was special;
      you are absolutely right.
Gazing at you makes me happy,
      and I look forward to more nights.
You have made every day extraordinary;
      you are the light in my eyes.
God has blessed me with you;
      my dreams I now realize.
No longer dreaming,
      you and I are together now.
I'm so glad to know your love I have found.
Thank you for making my dreams a reality.
Thank you for being the man who loves me.

This is a precious occasion,
      because two became one yesterday.
I look forward to growing old with you;
      we'll be together come what may.
I promised you forever with a wedding ring.
So, to your life it'll be nothing
      but pure joy that I'll bring.
This morning is so special to us;
      your smile is like the sunrise.
I'm so glad you're still here this morning;
      your presence brings tears of joy to my eyes.
I thank you for being the woman of God

who entered my life.
I thank you for not being afraid of commitment
    and for being my lovely wife.

No longer going through life alone,
because two became one
    when your love was shown.
You promised me forever
    by placing a ring on my finger.
By giving up the single life,
    you are no longer a bachelor.
Waking up this morning,
    seeing the look of love in your eyes,
brings a smile to my face,
    laughter to my heart.
    Your love gives me butterflies.
Thank you for being the man that you are.
Because it made my life easier
    when I gave you my heart.
Happily ever after is the life I promise you, because nothing
can change how much I love you.

Love For a Lifetime
Written April 23, 2012

Every time I see you, I melt like butter.
Sure, I have women friends,
    but you are like no other.
You're so delicate like a calla lily;
    how can I not love you?
Not just because of what you are to me,
    and the things you do —
though, I can't resist the way your lips caress mine —
I'm thankful that we're in love,
    and it gets better with time.
I just want to take my time with you and
    not just give you a five-minute sensation.
You are my wife and heaven's gift to me,
    and I want to shout that to the nations!

Each time I'm with you, my heart skips a beat.
I'm thankful; for the moments we share
    convince me I want something concrete.
None of my male friends can hold a candle to you.
I've been waiting to see when it will be just us two.
I've been waiting for some time
    to hear those three special words.
Not I need you, not I want you, but
    I love you —
    from this moment forward.
Give me your time, as I give you mine.
I want this love to last for a lifetime.

This is more than a physical love
    that I have for you.
We are so committed to love
    and know that God will see us through.
He is the third cord in this relationship,
    and I am so grateful for this love.
You are the only woman

who makes my heart fly like a dove.
My female friends don't
come close to your matchless personality.
You don't have to wait any longer;
your dreams are now a reality.
I will declare in front of everyone,
"I love you from this day forth."

I thank God for bringing you into my life.
No longer do I feel the trials and tribulations
brought on by strife.
Showing me the love only my true lover can give,
my heart beats; my breath quickens;
everything about you holds me captive.
There's not another man in this world
who holds my heart.
I knew that you were special from the start.
Thank you for making my dreams a reality.
Let's explore this love together;
we have no boundaries.

You're The One For Me
Written January 9, 2013

It's time to stop pretending
*   and time to admit the truth.*
We have been doing this for years;
*   we are no longer in our youth.*
You're the one for me; I can admit it now.
I'm just not sure where we go from here;
*   you haven't uttered a sound.*
You tell me you love me, but now that you have me
*   you don't know what to do.*
You have me wondering if you really loved me, too.
I can tell you now that you're the one for me.
*   I'm not afraid anymore,*
but your actions have me convinced that
*   you're not sure.*
You're the one for me, and I'm the one for you.
In time our love will be enough to see us through.

I'm tired of the games too;
        I so want to make you mine.
I refuse to let you get away, 'cause honey,
        you're so fine.
You're the one for me; my heart belongs to you.
I haven't uttered 'cause I wanted to be
        sure you loved me too.
Most attractive women already have a man,
        and I don't want to be a fool.
If I give you my heart,
        I just ask that you "don't be cruel."
I know you're the one for me,
        and I'm glad you see it, too.
Don't want you hanging on a string,
        now this love's for you.

Sweetheart I want you to be sure that
*   I'm the one for you,*
Because from this moment on
*   I refuse to play the fool.*
I fully intend to spend my life showing you

that I love you.
No need to worry; to you I could never be cruel.
I knew the moment I met you that
        you were the one for me.
Darling, I was just hoping there would come a time
            that you would finally see
our love for each other will carry us through time,
because you are my heart, you are all mine.

I'll be honest with you;
        I daydream of being with you all the time.
With all the men hanging around you,
        I'd thought I'd never make you mine.
So, what am I waiting for? Let me take your hand.
Slip on that wedding dress,
        and we'll walk barefoot in the sand.
It was my shyness getting in the way,
        and I've cast that aside.
If only my heart would stop beating fast,
        we could truly enjoy this ride.
Our love will stand through any test;
        it's now just you and I.
Now that our hearts have become one,
        let's just let our emotions fly.

Walking hand-in-hand, now husband and wife.
We have eternity to share;
        we have the rest of our lives.
I am happy that you have gotten past your shyness
        and are giving us a try,
because I am truly happy with us together,
        never having any reason to cry.
You are right;
        our love can withstand any test it is given,
because our love has been divinely written.

Taking A Chance
Written November 6, 2012

I'm so scared to get serious,
    but I feel so trapped inside.
I want to share my life with you,
    but my heart seems to run and hide.
There's a chance that you would be
    the one to break my heart.
I've been told to take that risk,
    even if you rip every fiber of me apart.
Experience is right, there's a chance for a heartbreak
    when you fall in love.
I'm tired of the relationships made by the flesh,
    it must be from above.
So, if I can keep you close to me,
    my heart will feel at rest.
And if I fall in love with you,
    will you catch my fall?
    For that will make me feel blessed.

Sweetheart, I understand being scared to get serious,
    to feel so trapped inside.
I understand wanting to share your life
    with someone but
    scared of the hurt that may arise.
There are always chances
    that someone may break our hearts.
But if we never try,
    we are doomed before we can start.
My emotions are difficult to explain;
    my heart is torn in two.
I know in my heart that
    I want to spend my life with you.
I'm willing to take that plunge to love you anyway.
All I can do is hope you don't hurt me,
    that here is where you want to stay.
Tomorrow is not promised to anyone;

so, it's time to take the plunge.
I am reaching out to you; please take my hand.
Don't you see that I am the one?

I can't believe
        you have my heart tied up in knots now.
I'll get through this without crying, somehow.
Your words touched the very heart of me.
I can get through my doubts,
        fears and personal frailties.
I believe I found an angel when I met you.
I will do my best not to hurt you,
        and believe me that's true.
Please be gentle with my delicate heart;
        I'm reaching for your hand.
Walk with me. Stay with me. Cry with me,
        for I want to be your man.

I do not have it in me to hurt you.
Every day I think of what the future holds,
        hoping you feel the same as I do.
Thinking of our days, our tomorrows, and our lives...
There is nothing I want more than to be your wife.
You are the man who has been sent to me,
the one man God knows who can and
        will make me happy.
I promise to be gentle, to love you with all I can.
Know you are special to me, my one-and-only man.

My friends always said if you're rejected,
        a broken heart can mend.
But most of them are miserable,
        and I don't like that trend.
I refuse to let that in my life; so I take this chance.
Lead me into the place
        where we dance our first dance.
I love you more than words can say.
I can't believe I just said that,

but I guess this was the day.
I promise to love you and cherish you for life,
and I'm a blessed man to have you as my wife.

I'm thankful for the day you were sent to me.
From the moment I met you,
I knew you were my destiny.
No more hurt shall be allowed in your life,
because from this moment on I will love you
completely for the rest of my life.
No longer thinking about the hurts of our friends,
we embark on our lives together
as we walk freely hand in hand.
I've never told any others
that they were the center of my world.
But know, you as my man, completed me
when you made me your girl.
Husband and wife is what we shall be.
Here, together, is where we belong;
we can make each other happy.

I love you, and that's all I can say,
and I will always love you 'till my dying day.

Even in death we shall never be apart,
because for now and always
you will have my heart.

It's Always Been You
Written April 24, 2013

*No matter how far away you may be,
I've always known you were the one for me.
It's always been you,
      even when we couldn't get it right.
Now is the time; our future is looking bright.
We have had plenty of obstacles;
      circumstances have gotten in the way.
But the love we have keeps bringing us together,
      our love is here to stay.
There have been times we couldn't get along,
but something keeps bringing us together.
      We could never stay gone.
No matter what others think, our love remains true.
I didn't realize until now how much I love you.
It's always been you;
      you've always been the one for me.
It doesn't matter if others are too blind to see.
A relationship is hard work;
      it doesn't always come easy.
Sometimes we run when things get hard;
      life is never easy.
Each day we discover something new,
but what will always remain the same,
      is how much I love you.
It's always been you; I'm able to admit that now.
That's never changed, no matter who was around.
I'm willing to take that plunge
      and see where this goes.
Nothing can get in the way and
      no one knows what the future holds.
From this moment forward,
      we will explore what is you and me.
The future has not been written yet,*

but we are each other's destinies.

I know you're so many miles from me.
I knew from the moment you kissed me,
     you were the one for me.
It's been you since the moment our eyes met.
My life was fine before meeting you,
     but I guess I haven't seen anything yet.
Love always finds a way back
     into these hearts of ours,
and it seems I daydream hour after hour.
We've had our share of ups and downs,
and it feels like at times
     I'm spinning on a merry-go-round.
It took some time for me to really see
     how much I love you.
People think I'm whipped,
     but my love for you is true.
It's always been you;
     there were times I was too blind to see it.
Friends can turn away from us; so be it.
I have a habit of running
     when something special comes my way,
but I still have
     to look at myself in the mirror every day.
I'm not afraid to admit
     that it's always been you.
Nothing can come between us,
     no matter what we say or do.
The future is ours for us to share.
Wherever you want to take our hearts,
     it's cool. As long as you're with me,
     I don't care.

I'm scared to be hurt again,
     but reaching out to you is what I do.
The only thing I know for certain is that I love you.
We have been going back and forth for

so many years now,
I can't imagine my life without you around.
Please, baby, tell me
        this time our love will see us through.
Please, don't make me spend my life without you.
Is love enough? Will it help us through our lives?
Is our love strong enough
        to keep us by each other's sides?
There is no other man in the world
        I can see myself with.
I have always thought a love like this was simply
        a myth.
Not a moment or a day goes by
        that I don't think of you.
Please tell me you feel the same way, too.
It's always been you, and it will continue to be.
We were made to be together; can't you see?

I guess that makes two of us,
        not wanting to be hurt again.
It seems like this is how most relationship begin.
We've had our share of heartbreaks,
        but I'm giving my all to you.
I agree, that after years of this,
        it's time for me to do what I have to do.
I want to spend every moment of my life with you.
To wake up beside you every morning
        is all I want to do.
I want you to be the mother of our children
        and I to be the father to them.
I'm drowning in the sea of love,
        and I have to sink or swim.
You're the only woman in my life,
        and this love for you is real.
I hope you can conclude
        that when it comes to you, this is how I feel.
It's always been you,
        and I want to be with you forever.

We are made for each other,
     and we both know that we belong together.

Knowing that we belong together is one thing
     but are you sure we can make it real?
I know that what we both feel is soul deep
     and very real.
Everything feels so unbelievably right with you.
I am trying to be patient
     and let you do what you do.
I know it's not the woman's place
     to make things permanent,
but I refuse to let you go,
     because you are heaven sent.
I have no problem letting you know how I feel
     and letting you know I need you.
No more waiting, no more hiding,
     it is time for it to be us two.
I hold your hand and gaze into your eyes.
You can see into my soul, and know I tell no lies.
I love you more and more every day,
and I know there is only one thing left to say.
You are my life, my world, the very air I breathe.
You are the only man in my life that I need.
     I go down on my knee,
Baby, will you marry me?
     Can you let down your barriers,
     and let me be the wife you need?

I'm sure we can make it real;
     you are my everything.
Although you're four seasons of my life,
     two stand out:
     summer and spring.
Love is truly in the air,
     and your wait is truly over.
So, put down the rabbit's foot
     and the four-leaf clover.

Love's Seasons

You are heaven sent,
        the woman who means so much to me.
So, it's my turn now
        to be the man I'm supposed to be.
You don't have to get on one knee;
        I was waiting for the right time.
Of course, the time is now to love you
        'til I run out of rhymes.
You are my life, my love, my sunshine and rain.
You are the woman
        who can erase away all my pain.
You are my best friend, my missing rib,
        a masterpiece from the sky.
I now get on one knee, and
        there's no one around except for you and I.
Will you marry me?
        I want you to be the wife that I need.
I want to be the husband
        that goes beyond what you can see.

Yes, my darling, I will marry you.
You are my light, my heart, my love is for only you.
No more guessing, no more running;
        It's now time for you to see.
You are the love of my life and you complete me.
We have both come to our senses
        and stopped hiding from what we know.
This love is the real thing,
        and a life together is inevitable.
You are the one for me;
        I want to shout it from the roof tops.
My love for you has grown;
        it's something that can never,
        and will never, stop.
You are the one for me.
You are my true destiny.

Committed To Each Other
Written July 14, 2013

What God has joined together,
　　let no man put asunder.
It's sad to see marriages today going six feet under.
As I look into your eyes,
　　I think about every up and down
　　we've weathered.
And I know I'm so blessed,
　　'cause we're so determined to stay together.
Honey, so many people don't want to try today;
　　they'd rather take the easy way out.
We both are so committed to live out
　　what a real marriage is all about.
I know getting here was hard;
　　thank you for telling us
　　to leave our past where it needs to be.
We are so committed
　　to make this relationship last until eternity.

Through our ups and downs
　　we have kept our faith present.
Without God in our lives, survival of our
　　relationship would have been absent.
Despite our pasts,
　　our lives were meant to be together.
Any and all storms our faith and love can weather.
Sometimes, I wanted to quit, just to walk away.
But then I looked in your eyes,
　　and something there convinces me to stay.
Love, relationships
　　and marriage have moments that are hard,
but nothing worth having is easy;
　　we must work diligently;
　　we must go that extra yard.

I think about what we went through,

and there were times I didn't want to try.
But the urge to stay committed
      was stronger than quitting,
      and I couldn't kiss our relationship
      goodbye.
Too many relationships have lost their spark.
      Just knowing you're with me
      every step of the way
is heavenly, and I know that I love you
      more than words could ever say
I am committed to your heart,
      your career goals and ambitions.
I am always astounded by your wit,
      personality and intuition.
Faith in the Lord is
      what keeps our relationship together.
With Him, we have a three-cord relationship,
      now that confirms our relationship
      will last forever.

You are my heart, but I admit;
      there have been moments
      when I didn't want to try
I loved you, and still love you so completely,
      that all I can do sometimes is cry.
This union means everything to me;
      never will I say good-bye.
No matter how hard it gets,
      I will always do what I must and try.
Being faithful to each
      other and always telling the truth,
will keep our relationship committed;
      we will always get through.
I support all that you need and all that you are.
I am right by your side, whether you are near or far.
I agree; our faith in the Lord
      is what holds us together.
I had to seek him first

in order to see our happily ever after.
You see; your heart was with Him,
    and through Him I was lead to you.
Our hearts are now one, and I can honestly say
    I love you.

I think of all the wrong I've done,
        and I ask that you let me erase that
        from your mind.
I wasn't being the man I know I could be;
        I was your rain instead of your sunshine.
You complete me in multiple ways;
        what else can I say?
I promise to make emotional deposits to your heart
        each day.
I am committed to being faithful to you;
        no secret bone will be inside of me.
When I put you down, I put myself down;
        when I see you bound,
        that means I'm not free.
You are in me, and I am in you;
        you're my best friend and my spouse.
You know, when we've fought,
        I'm so glad I never left the house.
I remember the day you got saved,
        the day we went out on our first date.
I made a vow to be a man, keep my commitments
        and never be late.
I pray for marriages, that they will last forever,
and that they will commit (like we do),
        through the ups and downs to stay together.

I love you — three simple words that mean so much;
But they are not just words,
    They are also expressed with your touch.
You have touched my heart
    and made a home for yourself there.
Trust me, Sweetheart, I'm never leaving.

I am not going anywhere.
I pause and glance around at the people
      who talk and stare.
No one knows our triumphs;
      no one knows why we care.
There will be difficulties
      and times we want to run away.
Nothing and no one
      can come between this love we share;
      our commitment is here to stay.

But no matter what, I've got you, and you've got me,
and that's the way true love is supposed to be.

A Blessed Union
Written December 11, 2016

I'm so blessed that you're in my life,
    and you're worth fighting for.
As we approach a serious relationship,
    fear is knocking at my door.
I know I have some flaws,
    but you love me anyway.
I know your life has been rough;
    So, here's what I'd like to say,
I won't promise you a flowery relationship,
    but I'm with you through the joy and pain.
Yep, like the song says,
    this will be like sunshine and rain.
If I ever trip, you can call some of my brothers
    to have them correct me.
But of course, you're my first human counsel,
    can I count on you to check me?

A relationship is built on give and take.
No need to run to others,
    when communicating with each other
    is what it takes.
From time to time we may get off track,
but I am here to tell you, with you is where I am at.
There is nothing in this world that can tear us apart.
Just as long as you remain loyal
    and faithful from the start.

Thank you for the assurance;
    I believe in communication.
Allowing ourselves to be transparent can allow
    what's hurt to bring healing and restoration.
Sadly, many don't want
    to go through adversity together.
But with this ring, I'm committed to you
    for always and forever.

I understand that the rough patches in our
      relationship are part of the vows
      and the process.
But if we stay focused on
      the promise of a blessed relationship
      in Him, we will have good success.
I appreciate you, and I promise to be loyal
      and faithful to you.
So how would it make you feel if
      I carried myself like I'm supposed to?

Of course, I want you to carry yourself
      the way you are supposed to.
We are at the point where
      we must do what we have to do.
Just keep in mind I want you
      to be who you are meant to be.
You are supposed to be the man who
      compliments and completes me.
As long as what you are supposed to do
      is also what you want to do,
      we will have no problems.
We must always be honest with each other;
      that way our love will continue to blossom.
When I told you
      I love you, I meant what I said.
Those aren't just words to me;
      they are a testament to what lies ahead.
Tell me, sweetheart, are you all in?
Are you sure you are ready
      to be more than just my friend?

Before I answer your question,
      I want to say something
      that might sound strange.
When I take your hand in marriage,
      I'm not marrying potential
      or someone I want to change.

I want to marry the woman
      who is standing in front of me,
      flaws and all.
Just as I want you to marry me, as
      I stand across from you proud and tall.
Am I sure that I'm ready
      to be more than your friend?
Does giving you the best that I got
      say that I'm in it 'till the end?
So, Baby Girl, am I all in?
      I'm as sure as my name is Tremayne.
So, let's take this spark of love that we have
      and turn it to a beautiful flame.

I love your words; they mean the world to me.
I'm absolutely ecstatic that you see what I see.
I've dreamed of the day that I would get married.
I knew I was sure, but I doubted you were happy.
Thank you for ending my misery
      and being honest with me.
I can now relax
      and rejoice in what you are giving freely.
You are my best friend, my heart, my soul.
Our future is bright; you have made me whole.

Destiny
Written April 15, 2018

Through the ups and downs and obstacles,
*   we know this is real.*
It's not something physical
*   but a deep emotion we feel.*
It has been preordained, written in stone.
As long as we stand together,
*   we will never be alone.*
No matter where we go, we make any house a home;
The love we have for each other is clearly shown.
You are my destiny; this I cannot hide.
*   The place I belong is right by your side.*

One of the reasons why our love survived,
is because we declared war on divorce and determined to
keep what we have alive.
We know that this destiny is not about us;
        there's more involved.
And to think, God didn't fix our marriage,
        He gave us the tools;
        so that our problems can be solved.
This love is real,
        and I believe it's to show the world
        it can be duplicated.
It doesn't have to be impossible,
        unattainable or even complicated.
You are heaven sent,
        someone I vowed to love forever.
You are my destiny, one worth fighting for;
        So, let's "Al Green" and stay together.

Telling you I love you every day;
tomorrow is never promised; so
*   I will keep it that way.*
I will continue to love you,
*   my sweetheart,*

my destiny.
I'm honored to know you show the world
how much you love me.
My baby, my heart, my love,
you are absolutely right.
This love has been sent from above.
God wants us to get it right,
to show others how it should be done,
to show that divine love is for everyone.
Staying together is imperative;
it's the only outcome I will allow.
Loving you now and forever, this is my vow!

Interlude #1:
Stephanie's Season

Rainy Morning
Written May 15, 2012

It's a rainy morning, and I have you on my mind.
I wish we were together, now; so, we could relax and unwind.
As I sit here, no work gets done,
As I reminisce about you and all your actions, my love for you
                    runs true and deep.
It keeps me up at night;
       don't know when next I will sleep.
I love you, I want you, and I need your near.
As I sit here on this rainy day,
      I wish you were here to dry my tears.

You and I know we can't go backwards;
      we can no longer be friends.
I really don't want to be the one to say this thing
      we have must end.
On this rainy morning, I can't help but wonder,
      What happened to us?
      What was it that pushed us under?
As I sit here, I wonder, what happened to our love?
I need some guidance;
      I need some insight from above.
I need to know what I should do.
Do I stay to work it out, or do I leave you?
I want to know when my rainy days will end.
I just want to be happy.
      I'm just not sure where to begin.

On this rainy morning, I have you on my mind.
Please let me know if this will work;
      please give me a sign.
Will we walk away alone and in defeat?
Or can we correct what's wrong
      and make each other complete?
On this rainy day, I think about you.
I'm sitting here wondering, will it ever be us two?

My Own
Written April 20, 2012

Always holding my own,
      never asking you for a helping hand.
Knowing that you were never there for me,
      I see where you stand.
Through God's blessings, I have become a success.
No longer wanting you around,
      I don't need nor want the stress.
You are all about yourself,
      never thinking about anyone else,
Yet you want to be around
      to bask in another's success.
You tell all who will listen
      that you made me who I am today.
I no longer care what they think;
      you have no idea
      what has made me this way.
You never knew about my trials and tribulations,
the mental and physical abuse
      that threatened to test my patience.
All I wanted was some understanding,
      but understanding comes from within.
It's my faith in God and his love for me
      that has helped me transcend.

You May Not Know
Written September 22, 2012

You may not know
      how much your heart can handle
      until you know loss.
You try to hold yourself together at any
      and all costs.
You must keep in mind,
      your faith will see you through.
Just trust in God; He has his hands on you.
I know it's hard right now;
      you don't know which way to turn.
Letting go of your father is not easy;
      It's something we are never prepared
      to learn.
      You will miss him; it will hurt,
      and sometimes you will cry.
You may even find yourself asking why.
He is resting now, no longer in pain.
He's gazing down at you your life;
      It won't be the same.
You may not know just how strong your heart is,
but you are a child of God; your faith is strong.
      He will see you through this.

The First
Written July 14, 2018

Let me be the first one you choose to come home to,
      the one who is on your mind all day and has you
      hurrying home, because you want to.
Don't care about the ones before me,
      because our love is real.
I'm the one you can't be without, the only one
      who makes you face what you feel.
Going through life attempting to figure out
      who you are,
while I'm patiently waiting for you to realize you've
      always been a star.
Let me be the first to tell you, you can be anything
      you want to be.
I'm just waiting for you to see in you
      what I see.
Through all the misunderstandings, the arguments and tears,
      there's nothing we can't face, nothing we should fear
Wrap your arms around me, and hold me near.
      Our future is bright, as long as WE don't let
      others interfere.
Let me be the first to say I will love you through it all.
Just remember, I'm holding you down; so don't let me fall.

Round and Round
Written July 12, 2018

'Round and 'round you go; where you will stop no one knows.
Being pulled in multiple directions praying for strength,
        so the hurt doesn't show.
Pretending to be okay, when you're broken inside,
trying to keep the tears hidden deep inside,
there's always something, always some excuse, always a
        reason you do what you do.
But the simple truth is, you care for no one, not even you.
'Round and 'round, back-and-forth games you play,
        Never once stopping to reflect on the hearts and love
        you've thrown away,
Always looking out for self and your own selfish needs,
not stopping to think about the person you've
        turned out to be.
'Round and 'round you go, not caring about your loss.
You only care about what you want and need, continuing
        to get it at any cost.
One day, you will wake up and realize what you need
        and love is gone.
One day, you will wake up and realize you're alone,
        all because you are wrong.

Interlude #2:
Tremayne's Season

What Went Wrong?
Written June 21, 2012

When I said I loved you, it was for real.
I put my heart on the line
        to let you know how I feel.
Now that you've left me, I'm on my own.
I can't take the feeling of being alone.
You know I think you're beautiful;
        you are my sunshine.
I wouldn't lead you on just to make you mine.
I want to earn your respect and friendship;
        without it I'm lost.
If it means giving up my life for you,
        I'll gladly pay the cost.
If I told you that you were special to me,
        would it mean anything to you?
Telling you pretty lies is something
        that I just don't do.
What did I do to cause you to turn from me?
Knowing that we're not even friends
        has caused me pain and misery.
You don't have to forgive me,
        if I have done you wrong.
I admit to you and the world my faults;
        with you is where I belong.
If I could just hold you and comfort your tears,
I'd let you know God loves us both
        and we have nothing to fear.

Now I'm alone, scared to even be alive.
No one hears my cry, how am I to survive?
Yes, I know the Lord, and He hears my cry.
Asking someone to pray for me,
        it's well worth the try.
Even if I'm rejected and am told to pray for myself,
I guess I just need Jesus and nobody else.

Why should people care if I lived or died today?
Everyone's happy but me;
    there's nothing more to say.
I will keep living,
    though I am traveling this road alone.
What went wrong?
    Can somebody just ring my phone?
I don't want to sound selfish,
    but I want to pray for you
    when you're in trouble.
Believe me when I say that
    I'll be there on the double.
But for now, I'm her enemy,
    and she's kissed our friendship goodbye.
No one cares about my heart; so a part of me dies.

Revelation of My Heart
Written June 22, 2012

You had my heart ever since our first conversation.
It was so hard for my heart
        to experience this revelation.
Our phone conversations could last an entire day.
We could reach each other's minds
        without a word to say.
From the first hug,
        I knew a friendship would emerge.
I still believe you're the one for me,
        and I feel this urge
to write this poem to you,
        because you are the one I adore.
When I'm in your presence,
        I know you're the one my heart beats for.

When we're away from each other,
        I don't know what to do.
I know fear is of the devil,
        but he wants to keep me away from you.
You enrich my heart, making me a better man.
Whether I'm praying for you or vice versa,
        I'm committed to serving you the best I can.
I know at times I feel disrespected
        when you turn; you don't listen to what I say.
And I know you feel unloved
        when all your needs aren't met every day.
Just say that we'll be together, and we'll never part.
For you have sent a revelation to my heart.

I would hate to see another man
        sweep you off your feet.
Exalting himself as a god,
        hurting you with lies and deceit.
I know men are disobedient, so full of pride.
When it comes to you, you will never have to worry

about me leaving your side.
If our friendship ends, so does my life.
I wish I could heal your bruises,
    relieve all your pain and strife.
I would hate to believe that I lost you from the start.
Because when I met you,
    you caused a revelation in my heart.

Dedicated To My Flower
Written July 6, 2018

I believe Anita said that some dreams come true.
The truth is, I found a real dream when I found you.
I know your youthful world tumbled down on you,
and no one but God heard them, as He redeemed you from
        hell and death, too.
One of the things that grabbed my attention about you
        was your heart.
That's where your spirit lies, and it told me you were special
        from the start.
Not only are you a woman, you are a daughter of
        the Most High.
To see how He's working in your life, I smile and, with joy,
        let out a sigh.

Many people don't know how to touch you,
        as you are a gentle flower.
Some will say sleep is your true freedom, but you found it in
        thanking Him every hour.
I count it an honor to have this flower in my life,
        and I promise to nurture this flower with no pain and
        strife.

This poem is dedicated to my flower, because everything
        about her is precious to me
If only I could pick her up from the garden to be mine,
        that would be a sight to see.

Love's Season #3:
Fall

Giving Love a Try
Written April 17, 2012

As my feet touch the Atlantic Ocean,
    my heart wells with tears.
Standing on the shore of Riviera Beach,
    wishing you were here.
Watching a dream slip through my hands
    does nothing to revive this dying man.
I go through life at times
    not wanting to face another day.
You may not know this,
    but my sunshine has faded away.
The sun, as it's setting outside,
    kissing this day good-bye,
leaves the feeling of emptiness
    and a spirit waiting to cry.

Sitting back wondering what is real
    and what's not.
Wondering if it's time to walk away
    from these battles we have fought.
You actions and words
    aren't giving me a reason to stay.
Your attitude is showing me
    that you are already on your way.
My day is dreary; the sun has gone away.
Now the two of us are hoping for better days.

I really don't want to say goodbye to you.
I need a miracle to make you stay;
    I don't know what to do.
I know my actions and words aren't perfect,
    but I do try.
I feel like singing falsetto, as it shields my cries.
Walking away rips my heart in two.
You are so special to me,

and I'm complete with you.
I know we come from two different worlds,
    but you are a special gem.
People are waiting for my demise,
    saying, "that's the end of him!"

You keep telling me
    you don't want to say goodbye.
But when I need you,
    you are never by my side.
I don't expect you to be perfect —
    just love me completely.
Honesty and respect is what I need to see.
No need for your heart to split in two.
Just show me you love me
    the way I love you.
Our differences are what makes us unique.
I enjoy knowing that
    there are things about you for me to seek.
No need to worry about what others have to say.
Just give me a reason that entices me to stay.

Let me stop for a moment;
    so, I can listen to your heart.
You have my undivided attention;
    square one is where I need to start.
I know I'm immature when it comes to love.
I know, and God knows,
    you're the only one I'm thinking of.
I want to love you the way you love me.
Whatever it takes, I'm willing to do;
    "only lip service" is not my cup of tea.
Can I promise you forever,
    or will my actions be enough for you?
I want to be a man with a backbone
    and to man up to make this love true.
If you are willing to listen to my heart,
I guess I can give an inch

and give you another start.
It's not that complicated; there's not much I ask for.
Just give your heart willingly —
     don't act as if it's a chore.
A relationship is something we must work at.
It will remain solid
     if we put in the time to ensure it lasts.
I need more than words.
     I need your actions, too.
Please give me a sign,
     some type of clue.
I want to believe that your love is true,
     I want to believe that you want me, too.
But, I'm not sure you realize
     how deep my love runs for you.

From this day forward,
     let's have a lunch date on Friday.
This is for us to communicate.
     I want to hear everything you want to say.
The good, bad and ugly;
     'cause the better I am to you,
     the better I am as a man.
I will give my heart to you
     every moment of my life
     and anything else I can.
I promise to listen to your heart,
     because it's everything to me.
When your heart hurts, mine does too;
     it's so easy for my eyes to see.
I know you love me for the fact
     you're still talking to me.
My love is true, and it's time
     I show you how deep my love can be.

I can't wait until Friday,
     because communication is the key.
We must make the effort,

if a future we want to achieve.
The fact that
　　you're willing to put your heart on the line
shows me that your love and heart are mine.
Keep giving me your heart,
　　and I will keep giving you mine.
No love like we have you will ever find.
I'm tired of hurting;
　　I just want to be with you.
As long as you remain true,
　　I will continue to love you,
　　as long as you love me too.

I misspoke and meant to say every Friday,
but truthfully, we can start today;
　　I want you to have your way.
Thank you for your love and understanding;
　　I don't take it for granted.
Getting to this juncture for my eyes to see
　　was not the way I planned it.
I have no problems putting my heart
　　on the line for you.
When you love someone
　　like the way we love each other,
　　there's nothing that I won't do.
I agree, this love is so special to me;
　　I cry silent tears as I sleep at night.
I will remain true, in fact,
　　you won't even have to ask,
　　because I'm determined to make it right!

Together Again
Written May 8, 2012

I'm so confused and not sure why I'm crying.
If I said that I'm OK, you know that I'd be lying.
Wheat happened to the dreams we used to share?
Did we grow apart
      to the point that we don't even care?
Our fight was so petty
      over who was right or wrong.
We can work this out;
      just bathe with prayer and a praise song.
I know we're to be together, and honey,
      please un-break my heart.
It's hard to be strong
      when I feel my world is falling apart.

I want to hold on to you.
      I want to believe this time it's real.
But I am afraid to give you my all,
      because it's my heart you steal.
We go back and forth, never seeming to get it right.
I just want to be loved; I am tired of the fights.
At this point in time,
      I don't even know why we argued.
This going back and forth,
      going over the same issues...
All I want is to feel my heart is whole again.
Please tell me you love me;
      I need the truth; there's no need to pretend.

It's real, and
      I want to be in love with only you.
You've already stolen my heart;
      so that makes two.
I don't want to go back and forth with our fights.
I want us to be strong, mentally and spiritually,

in the power of His might.
I want a heart whole, just like you do.
I won't let a day go by
      without saying that I love you.
As each day passes, my love for you
      grows stronger than the day before.
You're all that I dream of, and
      I promise each day to love you more.

Each day our bond grows stronger,
      and it's you I want to hold on to.
Each day I realize how much I love you.
My life is not complete without you in it.
I can't let you walk away,
      because you and I are not finished.
My day is not complete without hearing
      the sound of your voice.
You don't understand;
      my love for you is my destiny;
it's never been a choice.
From this moment on, it's all about you and me,
because my life will not be the same,
      if it's not you I see.
I love you now and forever, and I always will.
I have given you my heart freely;
      it's no longer something you have to steal.

You are my everything,
      the woman my heart beats for.
When I look into your eyes,
      I see that I couldn't love you more.
Without you, my life has no meaning or reason.
This is why I can say to the world that
      I love you for all seasons.
Can I just take you into my arms
      and console your heart?
You are the only woman for me,

and we're not to be apart.
I give you my heart and anything you desire.
Your love is my destiny as well,
        and it's my heart that you've acquired.

You are my everything, and I am so glad I'm yours.
I love telling everyone it is you I adore.
I am thankful you have come into my life.
I can see now there could be no other;
        I am ready to be your wife.
I could no more walk away from you
        than I could stop breathing.
This is all real; there is no acting.
I don't need you to give me all that I desire.
All I need is for you to love me completely;
        so nothing else can transpire.

Let me get down on one knee;
        this is the time for our love to shine.
I'm ready to be your man;
        forever I am yours, and you are mine.

The answer to that question is yes;
        it always has been.
You have my heart in a tailspin.

Friendship & Love
Written July 30, 2012

I need to get a message
      to someone in my heart.
Her friends are controlling her,
      and are breaking us apart.
We've got a love thang,
      and we love each other so much.
When I close my eyes, I can feel her touch.
Her friends don't care about her soul
      and want her to stay lost,
but I care for her soul and
      will reach out to her no matter the cost.
I'm striving for a better life;
      she deserves that and all things nice.
I'm a man and all that,
      but right now, I need some women advice.

As a woman, I give this advice to you:
Just be by her side and
      let her know that you are there for her, too.
Tell her that you want what's best for her—
      even if that's not you.
She will open her eyes
      and realize you love her soon.
Misery loves company, and
      her friends are not her friends.
One day she will see you are there 'til the end.
If love is on your heart, and its real and true,
just hold on; you will receive your due.
You are a great man,
      always thinking of others' desires,
but I realize that you can also get tired.

Thank you so much for
      being delicate with my heart.
I felt such a calmness,

and your words didn't tear me apart.
I know she cut me off due to
    the controlling influences around her.
My world wasn't the same the day that I found her.
It hurts that I'm the only one who
    wants to see her spirit soar.
Maybe I need new friends,
    and that truth hurts to the core.
Her friends don't care about her;
    my friends only care about themselves.
This is what's wrong with this world; we're selfish
    and caring for no one else.

No thanks are needed; this simply is what friends do.
We are there for each other no matter what ensues.
I hope she realizes soon that no one can
    or should control her.
She is special, but until she sees it herself,
    you can be her armor.
When you are on the outside looking in,
    you can always see what's wrong.
Just remain the person you are,
    and continue to be strong.
Letting go of your friends may hurt you to the core,
but having people in your corner
    will mean much more.
Selfishness seems to run rampant;
    everyone's out for themselves.

I know this sounds silly, and granted,
    this is how I act.
She can break my heart a thousand times,
    and every time I'll take her back.
The scales need to be removed from her eyes.
She'll need covering
    when she finds out the horrific surprise.
I have to be strong, just like you said,

maybe discernment is key.
When it comes to having true friends,
    what you said is totally for me.
It's sad that we say we love God
    but despise the lost sheep.
If only we understood that what we sow,
    we will reap.

What we sow is what we reap
    is so prophetic of you.
Trust me; this woman will soon see the clues.
The blinders will come off,
    and she will see them for who they are.
Make sure you are near, be there for her, never far.
God is our Father, and he wants the best for us,
but sometimes we can't see what's good
    until we get lost.
He says give our problems to him and just let go.
Stop worrying about our sorrows.
Give this to him; stop letting it tear you apart.
For He knows what's truly in your heart.
If it's meant to be, then it shall be.
You must have patience and faith
    and be willing to really open your eyes
    to see.

I know I need to be patient.
    I fear she will yoke up with a man.
But this man will believe he will be a god,
    and she will be his helping hand.
Unfortunately, he will never be,
    and her work will be in vain.
Just like sunshine and rain,
    it's initially joy, but it'll be pain.
I have no problems letting go,
    though I see her through every song I hear.
And as I go through life, I cry silent tears.
To the world,

I'm to be a man who never has a problem.
And I'll hear "For your problems, you have God,
 and that's all you need. He'll solve them."

It's hard seeing what you work for,
 someone else to profit from.
But I must believe that if she is meant for you,
 there could never be another someone.
Being there for someone day in and day out,
makes you a special person,
 one who knows what the world is about.
Yes, as a man,
 you should give your problems to God,
but I also understand that
 this is still something that is hard.
You are only a man,
 and all problems you can't solve.
You must hope that people evolve.
I truly believe that we all need spiritual guidance,
for He is who keeps us in balance.
Find your center, find yourself, and let her go.
One of these days the right one for you will show.

Yes, we are to give our problems to Him,
 but human counsel is needed as well.
When we turn our backs on them,
 you could indirectly be telling them to
 go to hell.
I guess the hardest part is to
 move on without her in my life.
Especially when we both
 dreamed of being husband and wife.
Well, this is the price I'm paying for dreaming;
 it's come to an end.
Never again will I expect my relationships to
 go beyond the level of friends.
It's painful, I know, but this is the only hope for me.
With that, I set her, my life

and everybody around me free!

Don't stop taking advice
      from the ones you hold close.
For these are the people who know you the most.
It's hard, I know, to let go of what your heart desires.
But if that spark goes out
      or is not there anymore,
      you can't rekindle the fire.
The dream of being her husband
      and not just her friend
means that you are the real deal,
      and with the right one
      your love will transcend.
I know the feeling of loving someone
      but not being loved in return.
But I refuse to believe that it's me,
      that it's my concern.
Don't limit yourself to remaining just friends.
Trust me; sometimes good things
      must come to an end.
Let go of the pain;
      one day it will get better you'll see.
One day that true love will be there,
      and you will truly be free!

Too Good To Throw Away
Written July 17, 2013

They say that hard times can break up a good love,
even if you think it's sent from up above.
We had one fight,
     and we're thinking about letting go.
I thought our love was stronger than this;
     don't you know.
We have so many things going in our corner,
     like our faith.
We know we are for each other;
     we can't afford to say it's too late.
I don't care about who's wrong,
     and I'll beg you if I must to make you stay.
You complete me, honey;
     this is something we shouldn't throw away.

I agree we shouldn't throw this love away,
but please tell me how is it that I can stay?
We seem to have hard times,
     more and more each day.
How does this love survive
     if we can't keep the hard times away?
I love you; this is something that can never change.
You just need to figure out
     how to keep those girls in their lanes.
Keeping our faith so we can stay together;
I want us to be committed for ever and ever.

I hate having this extra baggage in my life.
     I thought I closed it when I was with you.
There are so many jealous girls who just
     want to see our relationship is through.
Since you're a part of me, we can put them both in their
     place.
That's why I have you with me,
     you're my heart,

and I want you to invade my space.
I know you feel frustrated when it seems
    that hard times are all we see.
I don't like taking my pain out on you;
    it's not healthy for you or me.
You're the angel
    who holds the key to my little heart.
I'll do whatever it takes
    to ensure our love doesn't fall apart.

Communication and time are key.
No longer will I think about the others;
    I want my mind to be free.
I love you, and this is enough to see us through.
No outside influence can keep me from you.
Together as one we can put all others in their place;
because we know that together we are safe.
No more feelings of hurt or insecurity,
our undying love is what pleases me.
there's nothing that can
    keep me away from you.
I can honestly say, "you had me at hello."
The look in your eyes and
    the smile on your face had my mind blown.
Never ashamed to admit how much I love you,
Knowing that these feelings appeared out the blue.
People may say, "Relax, just take it slow."
But none of them know what I know.
No one knows you as much as I do.
They are confused about
    how much you love me too.
I smile when I think about
    what you went through to convince me.
That being with you was the right thing,
    it just took a little time to see.
That what I was feeling from the very start, was the over
flowing love straight from my heart.
Turning off my brain

and letting my heart take the lead,
allowing my heart to show me
you were and are what I need.
I loved you then; I love you now,
and I will love you forever,
realizing that together we make each other better.

I didn't think I was in love when I first met you.
I was happy with the fact that I was sad and blue.
Everybody was telling me
    that I was head over heels,
but nothing would ever compare
    to the way you'd make me feel.
Your smile dragged my heart
    through the ocean's shore.
Just being with you is
    all I would ever want and more.
You made my heart go through emotions
    like fire and rain.
I now know that only
    your spoken words can ease my pain.
Maybe I'm too sensitive, but I know you love me.
You entering my world
    has made my dream a reality.
My friends are so confused
    about the love I have for you.
You sent my life through a tornado,
    but not tearing my heart in two.
This feeling you gave me is
    stronger than any hurricane.
Whenever I'm around you, I easily go insane.
I loved you then and now;
    you're my future
    and have re-written my past.
If we were to drift apart,
    I don't know if I could let you go that fast.

Loving you has not always been easy;
sometimes you make me wonder
        if you will ever be pleased.
You may have not known at the beginning
        that our love is real,
but I am here to tell you
        exactly how I feel.
I've known since the moment I met you
        that you were my future.
I knew that never could I love any other.
As I look at you, I see eternity.
Baby, don't you know it has been divinely written
        that it will be you and me.
As I said before, I will love you forever.
Our love is strong enough to see us through;
        our bond is strong,
        as long as we are together.

I don't know if I'll be pleased with my life.
Will we just be friends,
        or will you be my wife?
Do you remember the times
        I would fly to where you are?
Just to be with you,
        as we watched the snow fall
        and the beautiful stars.
It was at that moment that I loved you,
        but couldn't find the words to say it.
You are a beautiful poet; the words you say to me,
        my mind has to play it,
two or three times an hour,
        and now I have to say that I love you.
I know you want me to say that I love you;
so, can I take you out in the snow
        and tell you that I love you, too.

No one has the power

to know what the future brings.
I just know that it's your arms I seek when it rains.
I find myself thinking of you
      constantly throughout the day.
I pick up the phone to call you, knowing
      I have nothing to say.
It's your voice that brings a smile to my face.
Just the thought of you and all doubts are erased.
I know you are scared;
      these feelings are a lot to handle.
My love for you knows no bounds;
I will always be here
      to make you smile when you frown.
We are meant to be friends,
      because our friendship
      is the basis of this relationship.
Our time getting to know each other
      has been time well spent.
Never doubt the reason why I am in your life.
I am content to know that you have already
      thought of me as your wife.
I will not rush you,
      because I know this is our destiny.
Sweetheart relax, it has
      and will always be you and me.

Free to Love
Written January 22, 2015

This message is dedicated to everybody;
     listen to us tonight.
We need to come out of the dark and into the light.
If we are truly serving Jesus, our Lord,
Then there's no reason we can't be on one accord.
If you turn off the lights,
     you'll find we're all the same.
Any division that's in the world,
we only have ourselves to blame.
I'm a part of you, and you're a part of me.
If we're unified — one Lord, one faith, one baptism —
     people can be set free.

I've been told that what's done in the dark
     comes to the light.
I've always been afraid of what can happen at night.
I pray to God, daily, asking him to give me a sign,
a sign that lets me know that now is truly our time.
I've loved you for longer than even you know,
but sometimes your actions have me
     thinking I should go.
You tell me I am a part of you,
     and you are a part of me.
But darling, with our past, how can that be?

I will be the first to say that our pasts are a mess,
but we have a choice to look at the past as a test.
I've loved you just as much,
     and I've prayed like you.
There are times where I reason in my mind
     what to say and what to do.
You're right; what's done in the dark
     must come to the light.
People don't take that seriously;
     now is the time to get it right.

I know my actions are a bit out there,
    but I love you more than you know.
I want to speak words of life and love to you,
    because I know that I reap what I sow.

I know in my heart that I want a future with you.
I truly believe that my destiny resides with you.
I want to get beyond the past
    and focus on something more.
I just need to know you have let go of your ego,
    and it's only me you adore.
No longer listening to my friends; my focus is on us.
This can only work if it's love and not lust.
I know in my heart that the time is right.
I need to let go of my insecurities
    when you are not in my sight.
Letting go of the past
    and holding on to what might be,
I'm here for the duration; I promise I won't flee.

A future with you is what I want as well.
There's something else on my spirit that I must tell.
You hit it on the nail about
    listening to these so-called friends.
They're just looking to control my life,
    but I know their time with bothering me
    has come an end.
I'm so glad we're confessing our faults
    to each other;
    this shows that we can heal.
Like the old song goes,
    time has allowed us to reveal
the things that we need to be free;
    So, we can love each other.
With you as my woman,
    there is no need for me to look for another.

You are so right; there is no other for me.

There is no longer anything in the street
*   I need to see.*
Through our struggles and our ups and downs,
one thing has remained consistent.
*   Only you have the ability*
*   to bring my attitude around.*
There is no other man for me;
*   I just want to be with you.*

There's no other woman for me;
     I only want you, too.
May God bless this union;
     now I know this will be true.
Only death will come between us two.
     I love you!

Back To The Beginning (Taking It Back)
Written April 15, 2018

We've been together for some time, it seems.
In the beginning,
    you were everything that I could dream.
Now, what we have is so fragile,
    and we've known it for so long.
Where's the fight that we both had
    to keep this strong?
Now it seems like we're strangers,
    acting like we barely know each other.
The truth is, you're one that
    will never be replaced by another.
I pray that there will be some way
    that we show each other that we care.
So, let me hear your heart; please be open to share.

It seems my heart isn't in it anymore;
    things just aren't the same.
I've been wondering why we keep trying,
    when our emotions are on different planes.
Never doubt that I love you, because I promise I do.
It's just that things are different now;
    I feel like it's not just us two.
I want to go back to the beginning,
    when we pursued each other,
back to a time we couldn't imagine
    having any other lovers.
I want to make sure this house is also a home.
I want to know that we will never be alone.

You know; we can't keep going
    through the motions anymore.
It's time for us to do something different—
    never done before.
Are you ready? Forget the idea that

God doesn't want us together.
Let's take your advice and go back to the beginning,
    where we promised forever.
I know neither of us
    wants to be the first to say goodbye.
So, that's hinting
    that we should give this love another try.
Do you remember if we had a mission statement
    for our relationship?
If not, let's build one now,
    as this is mandatory for us—
    on the serious tip!

Back to the beginning,
    are you sure that's where you want to go?
You want to start over,
    do things that we have forgotten we've done
    when we weren't afraid to let our feelings
    show...
writing each other letters,
    making phone calls just to hear your voice.
Are you ready to do the things
    that made you my choice?
I miss the man you used to be,
the one who used to sing to me.
I'm not sure what our mission statement would be,
but I'm willing to work on it,
    if I'm really who you seek.
I just need to know one thing:
can you, can we, stand the rain?

Well, we can just look at the good and bad
    of what we've been through.
The key is to not dwell on it,
    but learn from it, and start anew.
I wholeheartedly believe,
    because now we know this,

our latter will be greater.
It's better to start working on this now
        and not procrastinate by saying, "later."
You ask if I can stand the rain;
        the key is to go through the rain.
As long as I have an umbrella,
        know that I'm covering you
        through the heartaches and pain.
I declare that I'm all in,
        being all the man you
        (and God) need me to be.
If my man of God can be this to his wife,
        then I want to make
        what you dream a reality.

Looking toward the future and what it may bring,
I'm so happy to know we haven't thrown away a good thing.
I'm putting my trust in you;
I know our God will see us through.

Love's Season #4: Winter

I Can't (Remix)
Written March 9, 2012

Since you came into my life,
        there's one thing that's remained true:
You have done something to me that
        I certainly can't undo.
I can't let you go no matter how hard I try.
Every time I think about walking away,
        I just break down and cry.
From the moment you said hello,
        you had my undivided attention.
And now, years later,
        I still wonder where the time went.
I can't fathom my life without you;
I know in my heart that the future is for us.
Our future has been written;
        it is divinely meant.
You are my blessing;
        to me you have been sent.
I can no longer pretend
        that my feelings do not matter.
If I don't speak up,
        my heart just might shatter.
"No guts, no glory," is what they say.
        So, I am going out on a limb
        and putting it out there today.
You may tell me no;
        tell me you don't feel the same, but
        at least I have the knowledge that my fear
        didn't keep you away.
I can't go on pretending like I do,
        but I won't wait around
        for you to realize you love me, too.

When you entered my life, one thing came to mind.
     I didn't think love for each other
     is what we'd find.
I can't let you go,
     no matter what people want me to do.
I cry almost every day,
     because I always think about you.
From our first conversation,
     under the shelter of my umbrella,
     walking you to your car.
After a month, my mind was in space,
     and you gave me a star.
I don't want to consider the rest of my life
     without you.
We both know the future is for us.
There's no question in my mind that you are
     heaven sent.
I treasure every kiss and special moment spent.
You can't say my feelings don't matter to you.
I'm still your man,
     though you break my heart in two.
I make myself vulnerable to you today.
     Even if you reject me,
     I hope you remember what I'm about to say.
I don't want to pretend, even if you decide to do so.
I am willing to die for you,
     'cause I love you.
That's all I want you to know.

How Can I?
Written June 11, 2012

Anything you want or need is here for the taking.
My feelings are evident; I have no time for acting.
How can I love someone this way and
        so completely?
When his actions show me something differently?
Your words have me holding on,
        thinking that things will change,
but as time goes on, everything remains the same.
That look in your eyes when you are with me
has me blinded to the inevitable
        and the truth I just cannot see.
How can I continue to love you,
        when you are the man that you are?
These feelings are confusing to me;
        this is all so bizarre.
From the moment I met you, I knew I was lost.
I just had to have you at any cost.
Neither of us is willing to change.
'Round and 'round we go
        continuing to do the same things.
How can I love you so completely?
It's because I know what you are capable of;
        I'm just waiting for you to finally see.
Loving you now and always,
but don't take for granted that I can't go away.

It's springtime, and I'm so in love.
If only you could see that
        you're an angel from above.
Your friends mean so much more to you,
but it's so easy to love you
        regardless of what you do.
How can I love you when you're breaking my heart?
Was this your intention,

104

when you kissed, me from the start?
I know my life won't be the same,
    if you say goodbye.
And though I'm a man,
    I'll lay down my pride and cry.
You set my spirit ablaze when you hold me so tight.
I'm not like the men you've been with,
    I want you for more than just one night.
How can I love you
    when your friends have more
    of a say about your life?
Don't let your clique be your guide
    as to how you should act as a wife.
We have something special,
    but your friends love drama.
They are living for the moment,
    settling for mediocrity
    and being a baby mama.
How can I love you when
    you're being controlled by someone else?
I want you to want me for yourself,
    because I surely want you for myself.

I love you the same today as I did yesterday.
I keep hoping that what we have between us is real
    and convinces you to stay.
You say I'm living for my friends
    and letting them lead me astray.
But it's not them that is keeping me away.
I love you; I show it in my actions,
    and you hear it in my voice.
But you're running the streets,
    and playing with your female friends
    has been your choice.
Pride can get in the way of something
    that could be beautiful.
I've let go of my mine. Loving you is what I need;

can't you see I'm able?
I hear you telling me you want me for yourself.
I need more than words;
        I need to be more to you
        than just someone treated like everyone else.

I am committed to putting my life on hold
        to make this work.
I know I don't deserve you,
        especially when I act like a jerk.
Just like I need respect, I know you need love.
A love that loves you no matter what,
        and that only comes from above.
I have no problems giving up my female friends; I'm not the
type for them anyway.
They could care less if I lived to see another day.
Can you hear it in my voice,
        that I will do anything for you?
Of course, there is one limitation, and that's
        me not giving up my spiritual views.
Trust me in that my heart is with Him,
        and I swallow my pride for you.
I hope I can show you by my actions how
        I can love you.

I could never ask you
        to compromise your spiritual views.
What God puts in your heart will carry us through.
The one thing I need that's nonnegotiable
is for you to love me completely,
        just let your love flow.
I'm telling you now, and I am showing the world
that there is no other; I can only be your girl.
I love you; this is something I need you to know.
No other man has caused me to feel like this.
        I'm with your forever;

there's nowhere else I want to go.
Your well-being means everything to me.
Everyone else knows this ;
*   it's finally time for you to see.*

Thank you, so many women want me on their level,
thinking I don't know how to worship,
        or they want me to serve the devil.
I will tell the world that you are my only girl.
My love will constantly grow,
        and my feelings will always flow.
I love you with all my heart and my being.
Close your eyes, and never let go of this feeling.
No other woman has wrapped me up before.
And Sade was right; I couldn't love you more.

Separate Ways
Written November 11, 2012

I sit and reflect where we are today.
I feel this poem inside me;
      so, here's what I want to say.
Why did what was right in our relationship
      become so wrong?
Were we weak, pretending to be strong?
We promised to be true to each other,
      honest 'till we part.
It just feels like my heart
      is being plagued with darts
thrown by everyone who didn't care about me.
Tell me what's on your mind; tell me what you see.

It's hard to speak of what's on my mind,
because looking within causes me
      to fear what I will find.
Sometimes, I think that we were just
      not meant to be.
With as many problems as we have,
      a future I just can't see.
There is something inside of me
      that wants to hold on to you,
but then I reflect on the times when we argue.
Is it me who you are drawn to
      and really need in your life?
I need an answer to this question,
      before I commit to anything tonight.

I struggle with fear as well; I'm sure you can tell.
It feels like my heart is plagued with this evil spell.
I need to rebuke it and be free, but I seem to agree.
It just seems like we're just not meant to be.
I want you to be happy, and I hate to see you upset.
It seems like

the past is something we can't forget.
If we're going to go separate ways,
       can we still be friends?
You'll always be in my heart—
       even if this relationship has to end.

A relationship is not always meant to be.
Sometimes two people
       just can't make each other happy.
My fear of losing you has kept me around,
but I do not like the look in your eyes
       or to see you frown.
I would be honored and excited
       to continue to call you my friend.
It means that in the beginning
       our friendship was real and shouldn't end.
Never could I turn my back on you.
I love you as a friend and no longer want to argue.

I'm so glad we can end happy
       and not bitter and mean.
Who knows what the future holds;
       it remains to be seen.
This isn't goodbye.
       I will always be around when you need me.
I want you to be happy and, more importantly,
       for your spirit to be free.

I'm thankful for every moment
       you have spent in my life.
For together we will be forever tied.
I know this isn't goodbye, only a small separation.
Who knows what the future holds,
       what will be our next occasion.
Just remember as friends
       we will continue to be in each other's lives.
My love for you will grow;
       you will always see it in my eyes.

Love
Written November 29, 2012

Love, a four-letter word
          that can mean many things.
To each person, it has different meanings.
When I say that I love you, it's true and its real.
It's not just a word, it's something that I feel.
In time, these feelings may change.
It's not anyone's fault; there is no one to blame.
Sometimes love is just not enough.
Sometimes two people just argue and fuss.
Our trials and tribulations should make us stronger,
but I'm starting to ask myself,
          can I do this any longer?
I love you; that's not a lie.
          It's a feeling and a statement.
However, I am asking myself, were we ever meant?

Love, simply L-O-V-E.
For some it's reality, for some it's pure fantasy.
When I say I love you,
          I am laying my life down for you.
With all the hurt you've been through,
          you may not think this love is true.
My feelings are real for you, always the same.
If I miss the chance to be with you,
          there's no one to blame.
Sadly, we argue over things
          that don't mean a hill of beans.
Can you, perhaps, tell me what all of this means?

I wish I knew the answer,
          wish I knew what this means.
Your actions have me wondering if things are
          really how they seem.
I love you, and I always will.
But my heart is telling me this is not what you feel.
I'm being honest, and I need an answer from you.
Do you really want it to be us two?
If this is not what you want, then let me know,

and we will remain friends.
There is no reason to go further, no need to pretend.

I know you're not a fool;
        why do I feel the need to pretend?
I wasted this chance with you; I feel so bad.
You were the best thing that I ever had.
The way I treated you, I will never love again.
How could I hurt the one I love,
        especially my best friend?
I'm letting you go,
        not because I found someone else.
I am walking away from "love"
        before it rips me from myself.

My heart is breaking, it is now in two.
I never thought that
        I would live my life without you.
You are my best friend,
        I never thought we would end.
I thought our love could stand the test of time,
        that we could transcend.
I don't know where to go from here.
All I can do is wipe away the tears.
I love you now, and I will love you forever.
I guess we are just not meant to be together.

I'm crying, too, because I love you as well.
If I didn't tell you the truth,
        my life would be a living hell
One day we will be back together.
I need to be mentally straight,
        to promise you forever.
In my condition, I'm not fit to love anyone.
You are still my best friend,
        and we can continue to have fun.
Since I'm being honest, I must say this, too.
You have my broken heart also,
        and I will always love you.

Another Statistic
Written May 14, 2014

I came home to find a note stating
        that you're leaving me.
I read it intensely, hoping
        that my eyes were deceiving me.
I should've known something was wrong
        when you started to ignore me.
I took second place,
        and your girlfriends came before me.
Just knowing that you left me
        and the love we've built over the years,
has made me the saddest man alive,
        crying so many tears.
Look at our marriage;
        can we just be a little realistic?
We're feeding into society's standards,
        only for our marriage to be another statistic.

I can't stay away from you,
        but we can't be together.
I really wanted us to have a happily ever after.
I love you with every part of me,
but I don't trust you
        and feel that you are lying to me.
As I sit here trying to dry my tears,
I'm attempting to keep my thoughts
        from running away with my fears.
I never imagined love would be easy,
but I never wanted it to consume me so completely.
I love you more than any words can explain.
I am praying to see the sun shine through the rain.
It's never been about my girlfriends
        and hanging with them.
I run to them when my world at home

is filled with mayhem.
Why stay in a marriage where there is no trust?
Tell me, are you here out of love or lust?

I don't know what more I could say
  to make you believe me.
The last thing I want to think,
  is that you would deceive me.
That's not being fair to you, but
  I gave my heart to you on a silver platter,
and now I'm accused of being untrustworthy.
  I guess now it doesn't matter.
I made childish mistakes,
  but I was hoping you would see
  the changes in me.
When I found the Truth, my past was truly set free,
but something from my past
  must be haunting your world.
I'm here for love and only love,
  but I can't see my life without my baby girl.
There's no need to ask what I did wrong;
  I guess I should have already known.
I'll willingly take a polygraph test,
  and I'm not afraid to let my feelings show.
Every time I think of you now, all I do is cry.
Yes, I'm a man, but
  it's painful to hear the word "goodbye."

I don't know how to say goodbye;
  I don't even know if I want to.
I know with every fiber of my being that I love you.
I'm trying to let the past go, but can't you see?
  It's our problems, presently,
that have me doubting myself
  and how much you actually love me.
I know as we get older,
  we learn from our mistakes,

and we sometimes change.
I'm trying to play my position;
    I'm trying to stay in my own lane.
I want to fight for us; I want to know it's real.
But can't you see, I need you to understand
    and acknowledge how I feel?
I cannot see my life without my lover,
    my baby boy,
because you are that man in my life
    that brings me joy.

If only you could read what's going through my mind.
Well, a whole bunch of confusion
    is what you would find.
I guess that describes our marriage:
    pure miscommunication.
We're misunderstanding each other,
    and that just fuels our aggravation.
Can we sit on the couch;
    so I can give you my undivided attention?
And no, it's not for sex,
    but I want to listen to you,
    and may I mention
that I want to hear the good, the bad and the ugly; so I can
be a better man.
You complete me; you have my back;
    so, I want to do whatever I can,
to be a better husband.
    So, I'll stop talking and for once be realistic.
Speak your mind,
    for I would hate for our marriage
    to be another statistic.

I am reaching out to you,
    giving you this second chance.
I pray that I am not being unrealistic
    by taking this final stance.
I will tell you how I feel, what I think

and my insecurities.
Just be open minded, and really listen to me, please.
I do not want to believe
    that there are other women in your life.
I am your best friend, not only your wife.
You should have
    no need for communication with others,
especially when they are actively trying
    to become your lover.
Can we sit down? Right here. Right now.
Can we really fight for us;
    is a second chance what I should allow?
I can honestly say that you are the love of my life.
I can't part from you;
    we must find a way through this strife.
I will go to counseling,
    rededicate myself to the Lord.
Just promise me you are all in,
    and you will come to me
    when you are bored.

Thank you for this second chance;
    this is why I love you so.
You're not like other women I've met,
    they'd quickly let me go.
I've got some fight left for this relationship;
    you know I've had to fight all of my life.
You're my best friend, but you are also my wife.
Many women have tried to get me,
    ever since I yoked up with you,
but they had their chance and blew it;
    you are my dream come true.
Most of these women are chicken heads,
    they're not happy with their lives.
If we were to survey them, they feed on drama
    like the Real Housewives.
I found my angel when I found you;

you are truly the love of my life,
and I echo you in that
we must find a way through this strife.
I will join you in counseling, not for show,
but I'm totally devoted
to this commitment of love.
I'm all in, and those who are watchers
will have to know
that this love is sent from up above.

We can no longer
think about those watching from afar.
It's time to do battle, no more wishing upon a star.
I'm dedicated to you, this marriage and our life.
There is nothing in the streets for me,
no longer needing the nightlife.
Too mature for drama, that is nothing I need.
With you I can be happy.
Without you my heart bleeds.
God sent you to me; I do not question his reasons.
You and I are together for the long hall,
not just for a season.
I am, and will continue to be, devoted to you
and our love.
Our life has been divinely written;
it was sent from above.

Second Chances
Written April 15, 2018

Here I sit on this ledge by the ocean
        re-evaluating my life.
Regretting how I treated you,
        as you were my best friend and my wife.
I was such a fool to let you share my bed
        and not my bank.
Now that you're gone,
        I feel like a car with an empty gas tank.
You took my breath away
        with each kiss you gave me.
And to have felt your breath on my face,
        never ceased to amaze me.
If only I had one more chance with you,
there would be so many things different
        that I wouldn't do.

You speak to me about what could be,
        but you didn't value me while you had me.
I was always second guessing, wondering why me.
All I wanted was for you to love me
        and treat me as an equal.
Instead, you had me out here playing the fool,
had me sharing your bed but withheld the bank.
Thinking you could control me,
        if I didn't have anything.
Now you want a do-over;
        now you want to show me what I mean.
Now you want me to believe
        that I am your queen.

That's the one thing I always loved about you:
your truthfulness and faithfulness,
        but I acted like a first-class fool.
I guess I didn't know a good thing until it was gone.
I have to watch my words, especially

since I heard these words from you,
    "so long."
I can't blame you for the way you are treating me.
May this be a lesson to men:
    we can't be treating women
    like they're property.
Why did I treat you as just a piece of tail?
    That was so foolish of me.
I've been seeing dreams of changes I need to make;
    can you give me a timeline
    to make them reality?

Truthfulness and faithfulness is
    what I thought we had,
only to find out you strayed
    when you got bored or mad.
A relationship, a marriage, should be a partnership.
You don't run to another when things get hard, because you
don't like how things went.
You want me to let my guard down,
    to trust you again,
but right now that is hard.
    You weren't just my lover;
    you were my best friend.
Now I find myself wondering
    if anything you said was ever true.
Now I am wondering
    why I should or could ever trust you.
Give me a reason to believe you have changed.
Give me a reason
    to believe things won't be the same.

Let me say that I don't want you
    to let your guard down.
You have every right to keep it up; especially,
    with how I took your heart all around.
I don't want you think

that I have immediately changed.
That's pure assumption, maybe even presumption.
Either way, to think that is strange.
This is why I want you to hold me accountable,
no matter if you're near or far.
I heard my man of God say that, as a husband,
I have to get a revelation of who you are.
You are a woman, with real feelings,
a helpmate and not just a playmate.
Don't rush to get back with me;
we both need healing in our current state.

I believe you are right; we both need time.
If it's meant to be,
we will find a way; so, we BOTH can shine.
We have invested too much to simply walk away,
but you need to find yourself before you can stay.
Never doubt that I love you; that has not changed.
But I'm not the same girl, I'm a woman reborn.
Never will I again be played.
I'm here to be your partner,
your backbone,
your heart.
You need to realize that I'm here for you
and not fight you; we should never be apart.
There's no need to rush, let's take our time.
So, you will always be mine.

Thank you, accountability is what's important to me.
I've been attending these men's meetings,
and they stress accountability.
I've got my five core brothers to keep me in line.
That way, I can show you in deed
that I'm yours, and you're mine.

How A Man Should Not Act
Written April 15, 2018

When I think of the woman that you are,
      I don't deserve you.
I have made some bad choices,
      lied to you
      and failed to live up to my promise
      to be true.
Because I failed you,
      why do I have the right to be insecure?
Treat you like you would step out on me,
      acting so unsure
about you because I'm operating in a spirit of fear.
You've proven to me time after time
      that you that you'd always be near.
I need to get my mind cleared,
      renewed and ditch the past.
I apologize for burdening you and myself,
      we have to make this last.

It's difficult to come back from infidelity;
Trust becomes an issue for all involved,
      because of what you thought was a need.
You don't trust me, and I don't trust you
      because of your actions.
The actions that caused
      these insecurities within us both,
      because we don't know
      if our love will be everlasting.
You want me to forgive you, to let the past go.
But when you treat me like I'm in the wrong,
      I'm not sure which way to go.
For some reason you felt that you needed another;
but now you claim you realize
      that there could be no other.
I've shown you time after time

that there's nothing more I want,
but your actions make me believe
    that you are still putting up a front.

There's a part of me that doesn't want
    to hear what you say.
I know you're telling the truth,
    but I still want to live my life my way.
Why do I have to treat you like this?
    Physically and emotionally abusing you,
giving you black eyes,
    knowing you'll stay—
    anticipating that's what you'll do.
So, why do I have the audacity to think
    I can have my cake and eat it, too?
It sounds like I'm playing you for the fool;
    in my mind, I know it's true.
I need your help, but to be honest,
    with my attitude,
    you shouldn't feel safe in my care.
I'm volatile, broken and in need of help.
    I ask for your help;
    I now listen to what you have to share.

Throughout all the emotional and physical abuse,
    you dare ask for my help.
You want me to give you all of me,
    never listening to what I have to say.
Why should I stay?
    Why shouldn't I run for the hills?
Why should I believe remorse is truly what you feel?
You are saying and doing whatever you have to,
    to keep me here.
Only because you are afraid to be alone,
    silence is what you fear.
It's been years and years
    that I have continued to love you,
but the only thing you focus on

is what you want to do.
I've finally found myself;
    I think I am ready to walk away,
and now you have decided
    you really want me to stay?

How can I blame you for walking away?
We don't trust each other,
    and you fear me day after day.
My actions have consequences;
    this is a lesson I need to heed.
If men can learn from this mistake,
    then they'll understand what it means
    when a woman's heart bleeds.
I have betrayed your trust, your love
    and all that you've done for me.
I now understand the cost of being selfish;
    it's plain to see
that I need to take stock of my actions
    and my words,
    and how they affect those around me.
You hold a place in my heart;
    while I go get counseling,
    I must face the truth.
    Only then will I be free.

Praying that counseling will be all you need,
hoping it's what you need to set you heart free—
you're my best friend,
    and I will never turn my back on you,
but it's time to focus on making you a better you.
Forget a relationship;
    let's just focus on being friends.
We never know what the future holds;
    who knows where this will end.
I'm hoping we are old enough

to learn from our mistakes.
Praying there's a better ending to our fate.
Call me if you need me,
        if you ever need to talk.
But right now, I believe
        you must be alone in your walk.

As a man, I accept responsibility,
        and I need to be alone
        for this part of my walk.
I do covet your prayers, as I'm in therapy.
        I want my actions to match my talk.
Thank you for not throwing our friendship away.
So, I say goodbye for now,
        and I know you'll think of me
        when you pray.

Happily Ever After
Written December 2, 2012

Do you believe in happy ever after?
In the days that our life brightens up
        because of our laughter,
I wake each day just to see your smile.
For you, my dear, I would walk miles.
Happily ever after may be just a dream,
but I know that to you my heart clings.
One day soon, you will realize
        you are my Prince Charming.
I'm your best friend, your heart, your love,
        your one-and-only, darling.
Do you believe in happily ever after?
Do you believe we are meant to spend life
        listening to each other's laughter?

Yes, I believe in happily ever after.
I believe in fairy tales with all the joy and laughter.
When I awake, I dream of you close to me
and the idea of becoming one, as we live so happily.
I pray you realize that you're my Cinderella.
Your work isn't in vain; it's fit for this kind of fella.
Let me share this happily ever after with you.
This carpet ride was made for us two.

You want me to believe in a fairy tale,
to believe that our love is real,
        and this is a great story to tell.
You want me to realize that you are the one for me,
but something is holding me back,
        keeping me from being happy.
I want to hold on to the hope that
        there will be a happy ever after with you,
but right now I just don't see how
        the future will be just us two.

124

I can understand, and I also know this reality.
I believe I'm mature enough to know that
        I can't make you love me.
I don't want you to believe in a fairy tale
        'cause it's make believe.
I'd prefer you believe in us,
        but I'm starting to perceive,
that you don't love me. I'm able to understand.
I guess we'll dream our lives away,
        as I wonder off as a lonely man.
I've seen this scene before;
        I don't know if you have as well.
It's rather depressing,
        and the feeling is like a suicide spell.

It's not that I don't love you,
        because believe me I do.
The problem here is that
        I don't believe you love me, too.
I used to believe in fairy tales,
but then my heart was broken,
        and my fantasies have been derailed.
I have waited an eternity for you
        to realize that my love for you was true.
Over the years I wanted to you to choose me,
but now I see that
        you aren't the person you pretended to be.

I won't sit here
        and make excuses for my multiple mistakes.
Don't feel sorry for me;
        this is a bitter pill I must take.
I love you, but I can't promise you forever.
This is hard for me,
        because I dreamed of us together.
I don't want live from dream to dream
        and then have it end.

With a life like this,
    my heart will never mend.
You deserve someone so much better than me.
I'm sorry to be immature and waste your time;
    I just want my spirit to be free.

We both were young,
    not understanding what we had.
There is no reason for either of us to be mad.
Sometimes love just isn't enough
    to keep two people together.
Sometimes it's just not strong enough
    to keep them together.
I love you now and I will love you forever.
My heart simply can't handle this stormy weather.
It hurts me deeply to say we have to part,
but I think we were doomed from the very start.
It's not about maturity
    or the mistakes that were made.
I believe that you love me,
    just not enough to keep up this charade.
Through all these years you never picked me,
I have concluded your heart knew it wanted to be free
without me.

It's not so much free without you,
    just wanting to be free altogether.
I just want my spirit to soar the heavens forever.
I thought love was what I wanted in my life.
I thought you would complete me as my wife.
It's not you;
    I can't take living my life like this anymore.
It hurts that I'm leaving like this;
    this pain is like never before.
Please don't cry that I'm leaving this way.
The real conclusion is that
    I won't live to see another day.

Don't talk like that; I never want to see you hurt.
We should have put our friendship first.
I'm here for you always and forever.
If you leave me today, there is no hope for better.
We may not be together, but I can live without you.
The two of us together may not be an option,
        but I still love you.
I know with all certainty that without you
        my life will never be the same.
I am the moth that is drawn to the burning flame.
Please, sweetheart don't say you have to go.
Let our friendship be what binds us together,
        even if our love doesn't always flow.

I'm trying so hard not to cry;
        I'm going to get help right now.
I'll find a way to cope with my life,
        someway, somehow.
I need some relief from the pain
        that I feel in my heart.
It feels like my entire world is falling apart.
I feel the love of God in the words you say.
Thank you, God, for sending an angel my way.
I will always cherish our friendship,
        and you're my friend for life.
Pray for me while I'm institutionalized,
        I know you're going to make a great wife.

I'm praying that you find the help you need.
The world needs your smile and your laughter.
        Don't you see?
My friendship will always be here for you.
This is a fact, and it will endure through any,
        and all issues.
Take the time to take care of yourself.
And think about me

when you feel there is nothing left.
Do I believe in happily ever after?
Yes, because through all the pain and tears,
*   I can still hear your laughter.*

All I can say is thank you and yes,
    I believe in happily ever after,
as well as in fairy tales,
        with all the joy and laughter.

Tremayne's Acknowledgements

First and foremost, I would like to thank my Lord and Savior Jesus Christ, for Your love, salvation and for carrying me through this project.

To my mom and sister (and her family) — I love you dearly.

Dad, though you're not here physically, you're here and living in my heart. I know you're proud of me, and that means the world to me.

Stephanie Tysor, ever since 2012, this book took form. Thank you for challenging me with your creative mind, and I'm sure I did a great job challenging you to expand your mind as well. Congratulations on your first work, now you know what this means (smile).

I want to also extend my sincerest gratitude to the following individuals (who have sown into my life):

Makasha Dorsey, I thank you for taking the time to edit this book and provide constructive feedback (smile).

Cynthia M. Portalatín, I thank you for copyediting this book. Of course, you know we have a friendship that extends beyond business. You know I'm still waiting on a follow-up to your book "Bloom Forever" (smile).

To my **Apostle and First Lady, Michael A. Freeman & Dr. DeeDee Freeman**, thank you so much for imparting into my spirit every Wednesday and Saturday. To all in my **Spirit of Faith Bible Institute Class of 2020**, we are family; enough said! I love you all, along with every instructor.

To my **Special Flower**, you know who you are; you are a blessing to me in ways words could never describe. You are so awesome, so special, and most of all, so beautiful to me. Page 76 says it all!

I would like to extend my appreciation and love to all of the ministries, church families, public and private schools, bookstores, book clubs, and different outlets that have supported my ministry.

To all who have been touched by my works, just know that I love you dearly and we're family. I've got your back, and you will always have a friend in me.

To all of the wonderful authors I have met over the years, I am forever in debt to you. Thank you for sharing your wealth of knowledge with me, and I pray much success in your careers.

To the **Tallahassee Authors Network** (TAN) family and **Tallahassee Writers Association** (TWA) family, you are truly my brothers and sisters in writing, I would thank you all individually, but there are too many of you, and I don't want to miss any of you (smile). The best is yet to come for all of us.

To all of my friends (past, present and future), know that I love you with all of my heart, and you are not forgotten. If I forgot to mention you by name, forgive me; I'm getting old (smile)! Charge it to my head and not my heart.

Stephanie's Acknowledgements

To all the readers, thank you for giving me the opportunity to express myself. I hope you read something that touches you profoundly.

Tremayne Moore, there are not enough words to express the thanks I have for you. You have been my friend since we were children and will continue to be my friend for life. I thank you for believing in me and taking a chance on me, even when I didn't believe in myself. You are an inspiration.

My life is full of people who have inspired me and given me the strength to pursue my dreams. To my family and friends, thank you for being in my corner and pushing me when I wanted to give up. I love you!

To all the people instrumental in getting this book out, thank you. I am new to all of this and still learning everyone's names and what contributions you have added.

To all of the readers (past, present and future), I hope you find something in your reading that touches you as much as it has touched me.

About the Authors

Tremayne Moore, founder of Maynetre Manuscripts, LLC, is an accountant, writer, psalmist, modern-day Griot, and Spoken Word motivational speaker. He is the author of the poetry series *"You Can Take It"* and the novels "Deaf, Dumb, Blind & Stupid" and "Pieces of Me." Academically, he holds a Bachelor of Science degree in accounting from Florida Agricultural & Mechanical University and a Bachelor of Science degree in management information systems from Florida State University.

Tremayne's life can be summarized with a quote from the Apostle Paul from the Book of Philippians:
"Christ shall be magnified in my body; whether by life or by death."

Publishing Inquiries & Speaking Engagements:
Maynetre Manuscripts, LLC
P.O. Box 1819, Owings Mills, MD 21117

Connect with Tremayne Online:
Website: www.maynetre.com
Blog: http://mayneman.blogspot.com
Facebook: http://www.facebook.com/AuthorTremayneMoore
Twitter: http://twitter.com/Mayntre
Email: tremayne_moore@yahoo.com

Stephanie Tysor, first time author, is an administrative assistant. Academically, she holds a Bachelor of Business in administration, general management from Bryant & Stratton College and a Master of Business Administration, with a specialization in human resource management from Ashford University.

ᏣᏳᏏ

Connect with Stephanie Online:
Facebook: https://www.facebook.com/tysor36
Twitter: https://twitter.com/MsBadness
Email: stysor32@yahoo.com

ᏣᏳᏏ

Love's Seasons

Made in the USA
Columbia, SC
13 August 2018